A GAME OF THREE HALVES

A Game of Three Halves

British Ice Hockey's Changing World

LIAM SLUYTER

MAINSTREAM
PUBLISHING

EDINBURGH AND LONDON

Dedicated to Mum and Tony,
who were fantastic when they were needed
– and cool when they weren't.
Love you both, obviously.

First published in Great Britain in 1998 by
MAINSTREAM PUBLISHING COMPANY (EDINBURGH) LTD
7 Albany Street
Edinburgh EH1 3UG

ISBN 1 84018 022 6

A catalogue record for this book is available from the British Library

Typeset in Berkeley Book
Printed and bound in Great Britain by Butler and Tanner Ltd

CONTENTS

A Tip of The Hat To . . .

Yet again, I'm going to have to mention a few people who helped me along the way, without whom this book would blah blah blah. Look, you know who you are, and what you did. Obviously you could have done a bit more to help, and really you don't deserve any credit at all, but I'm in a good mood today so you're going to see your name in print now (exciting, huh?).

Hockey People

Biggest thanks of all to the guys who took time out to be interviewed; cheers. Thanks for putting up with my stupid questions, and for not giving me boring answers. Hope you like your bits. Also – Nico Toeman for helpful phone numbers; John Lawless; Simon Potter for the jokes and info; the fantastic Joanne Houlcroft and Lara Lockwood for all the press releases and tickets; Julie Oldfield, once again; Harwood & Co; The ISL; Peter Adams at the Newcastle Arena; Keith MacGregor for the Devils stuff; Mike O'Connor at Sheffield; Stewart Roberts and his invaluable annuals; Ken Dryden and Roy MacGregor for setting the standard; Simon Buckley for the photos and being cheap; and Mark Jones, Keith, Peter, Martin, Chris and the rest of the Nynex press box posse, who'd better give me good reviews. Or else.

The Friends

Plenty of you helped out just by being around, so hugs and thanks to –

John Collett, the best; John Gaustad and the sportspages crew, even Dom this time; Bill Borrows for being, argh, just . . . Bill Borrows; Mark Goodwin; Wanda Sluyter (no relation); Bill Sluyter (who certainly is – cheers, Dad); Fred; Kris Whitehead, 'cos he wasn't mentioned first time and made a right girly fuss; Nathan for technical support; Julie for emotional support; Nick Catterall for all the hockey chat; Mark Swanwick; Tracy; Branwen; Gerry; Porl; Paul C; the Debster; Nikkism; Douglas H; Ant; Rich; everyone else at Loot I like; Amanda Clayson, who hasn't apparently done anything to warrant inclusion; and everyone else who I've forgotten, sorry, look, I'm tired. Music by Radiohead, Mogwai, The Little Things and The Junkword Engineers. I knew them before they were famous.

Finally, cheers again to the Mainstream gang, especially John, for again putting their money where my mouth is, and letting me do my thing.

About The Photos

All the photos in this book were taken by the excellent Simon Buckley – who worked for no gain other than to help a mate out, the chance to hang out at a few games, and the opportunity to occupy his boisterous daughter Mimi and be fleeced of a few quid at the same time. His work has appeared in the past in *Goal*, *Loaded*, *90 Minutes*, and a whole bunch of other magazines, but this is the first hockey book he has worked on. He is a Bolton Wanderers fan, but pays for it every day of his life.

Introduction

Hello you lot, welcome back. Those of you who have been paying careful attention will know that this is, in fact, my second hockey book. The first was *Seasons to be Cheerful*, also brought to you by the good folk of Mainstream. Read it? Well those of you who haven't, go and buy that before proceeding. I need the money. Trust me, you'll like it. It's a bit raw, perhaps a bit naive in places, but it's fun enough. The rest of us will just wait here for you to catch up.

Back with us? Okay, since I wrote it, and hardly any death threats have appeared in my letterbox, I have been thinking about whether I wanted to write another one – these things are very time-consuming, you know, and eventually, after much soul-searching, and the money from the first one had dried up, I decided that I did indeed want another pop. Hence the book you have in your hands now. The trouble was, what to write about this time? Now during the course of writing this, lots of people have asked me what it was going to be about, and almost without exception, they have assumed that it was going to be *Seasons . . . Part 2*. In other words, more of the same. This surprised me. If you've been lucky enough to get to write a book, and then civilisation hasn't collapsed and you've been allowed to write another, what is the point of duplicating yourself? Unless you're an Oasis fan, you're not going to want to hear the same things over and over again, witlessly repackaged. If you enjoyed the first one, and want more of the same, then fine, read it again. You'll have forgotten most of it anyway. Me, I wanted to move on. And so, it seemed, did the rest of hockey.

In the couple of years since I wrote the last book, ice hockey in Britain has moved on considerably – most obviously with the advent of the Superleague and the phenomenal jump in playing standards. From a writing point of view, all this change has made things tricky. Week by week, it seems that new players have arrived, old teams have gone bust, new ones have come in to replace them, and those new players I was just telling you about turned out to be no good and have been sacked already. Honestly, you can't keep up. It will be about a year between me starting to write this book, and you lot getting your grubby mitts on it. In that time, everything might have changed. This did cause a few headaches when it came to thinking about what to write about. For instance, what would be the point in discussing league organisation when I have no clue as to what shape hockey will take by the time you read this? What would be the point of moaning about the indifference of the London-based media to hockey, and the lack of a team in the capital, when this problem might have been resolved by the time the book is published? (In fact, it does now look like there will soon be a team in London. See what I mean?) How could I write a book that wouldn't be obsolete before it was even printed?

Okay, so you could argue that I could always look back and write about the past. In the last few years, hockey has changed almost beyond recognition in Britain – so why not write about that? Well, to a point, I have, but the trouble with that is that it is *still* changing. In a few years, when things have settled down a bit, we'll get a better sense of the direction the sport has moved in, and what needs to be done to improve it further, but in the midst of change it's very hard to see how things are taking shape. With this in mind, I decided to take a step back and try and write something that, although it would reflect all the changes that have hit the game in recent years, would also still touch upon some of the qualities that have always been the same. Hey, don't look so worried. All I did was talk to some people, a few players, a coach, a ref, a money man, that kind of thing.

The idea was to try and get a sense of the game from different perspectives, so that by placing them side by side you might get a sense of the game as a whole. To see how the game looks to someone who has seen all the changes, and to someone who has just arrived. To view the game through the eyes of a player, or an official, or a businessman. To talk about stuff specific to the game here, but to still see that it's just hockey. It's still the same game, with the same passions and the same hopes as anywhere else in the world. There's no particular point to all this, as such. I don't have any agenda here, so there's no grand conclusions. Just stuff I hoped was interesting to hockey fans. It's not perfect, there are certain teams that I would like to have talked about which I haven't, and perhaps some of the interviews overlap more than I ideally would have liked, but hey, you can try forever to write the perfect book and never get it finished. Or you could just get on with it and release an imperfect one. For now, this'll do. Hope you enjoy it. See you at the rink.

Liam Sluyter
Manchester, April 1998

Before We Proceed

It has come to my attention that some of you have been watching football when you should really have been watching hockey. So look, if we're going to do this properly, there need to be a few ground rules. (Those of you who know their stuff can skip this bit.) Firstly, it's not a ball, it's a *puck*. This means that encouraging shouts of 'Good ball' will not be tolerated from members of the audience. If you must show your appreciation for a good pass, why not try saying 'Good pass' instead. Go on, try it. See? It works just as well. Okay. Now I'm afraid you can't ask me what time kick-off is because the game doesn't have kick-offs, but face-offs instead. Like the film with John Travolta and Nicholas Cage. A minor point, sure, but one worth making. Now the goalie. This has been confusing some of you, and I admit it's tricky at first, but your options are: netminder, goaltender and goalie – so try and avoid saying 'goalkeeper', because that is incorrect. If you can manage to say defencemen instead of defenders then I'll be pleased, and to make things easier for you, a forward can still be a forward. Don't ask me how many halves there are, though – it's a toe-curlingly stupid question. They are called periods, anyway, and there are three of them. There is more, but I can see your eyes are starting to glaze over, so we'll leave it for now. I'm sure you'll be able to work out the rest as we go along.

Enjoy the book.

FIRST PERIOD

A Tale of Two Cities

In a football-worshipping country such as ours, it is regarded as an act of heresy to suggest – as I have often done to various bemused friends and colleagues – that ice hockey is 'The Greatest Spectator Sport in the World'. I have always been deadly serious when I have said it, but the response I have tended to get is the kind of facial expression that I imagine Jehovah's Witnesses are used to seeing on peoples' doorsteps, as their victims slowly register the fact that something unspeakably grim is about to happen to them. As a way of impressing strangers it ranks right up there with showing them your membership card for the Flat Earth Society. This in itself would not really be a problem were it not for the fact that, crucially, *I am right*, and *they are wrong*. I'm preaching to the converted here, I know, but we would do well to remember that for the vast majority of the British population ice hockey is as important to their everyday lives as heavyweight boxing is to goldfish.

With this in mind, the recent success of both the Sheffield Steelers and the Manchester Storm, in attracting the kind of crowds to ice hockey that had hitherto (outside the Wembley championships) been unheard of, takes some explaining. In the 1997/98 Superleague season, these two teams alone accounted for almost 54 per cent of the audience the sport attracted at the top level. Why? Sure, part of the reason is undoubtedly the obvious one – that they simply play in buildings that are that much larger than their rivals', but there is more to it than that. Both clubs had to sell the game to a mass audience, and whilst neither has been without its critics, by and large they have been successful in this. How? The answer is not straightforward by any means, but undoubtedly part of the reason is the marketing.

This may be anathema to some of you, but the truth of the matter is that you simply can't let a bunch of guys dash around a patch of ice routinely clobbering each other and expect thousands to turn up to watch each week – well apart from in Kirkcaldy. Alas, you have to cajole people. Educate them if you like. Obviously, some people will turn up regardless, the die-hard fans who are so besotted with the game that they would turn up in their hundreds just to watch the Zamboni clean the ice, but the trouble with this group, and I sadly am one of them, is that there simply aren't enough of them to ever fill the kind of arenas that Manchester and Sheffield have on a weekly basis. To an extent, when you launch an arena team you don't really have to pander to the die-hards – they'll come to games anyway. Sure, they'll be the ones who are first to complain about the ridiculous prices charged for beer, or the first ones to point out which players have obviously been signed by mistake and should be bundled into a large crate and shipped back to Saskatchewan, but they'll also be the first ones back next week. It's the other people, the ones who haven't made their mind up about the game, the ones who won't necessarily complain if something's not to their liking, you have to worry about. If they don't like it, you simply won't see them again. And that's assuming that you were somehow able to lure them to the match in the first place.

So when, in 1991, Sheffield Arena opened its doors and it was announced that the Sheffield Steelers would play there, it was quickly realised that to fill the 8,500 seats, they wouldn't just have to attract ice hockey fans, they'd also have to attract people who were barely even aware that the sport existed. To find out how this was done, I chatted to one of the guys entrusted with the job of doing just that, Dave Biggar, who would later go on to repeat the success – although not quite the method, at Manchester with the Storm. Biggar's background was not in sports but, tellingly, in entertainment, and despite the fact that he knew nothing about the game initially, he was staggeringly successful, although only after an admittedly sticky start . . .

'We worked 24 hours a day,' he recalls. 'We came up with the name, came up with the logo. Sat down, worked out the programme, worked out the ad campaign, sorted the tickets out, put the whole thing together, tied up the radio deal, sat down and worked out a basic entertainment programme.' And the result of all this hard graft? 'The first game kicked off with, I think it was, about 300 people, most of whom had got complimentary tickets – we issued thousands of comps, but only 300 turned up! We just sat there and thought, "What a miserable start . . ."' For a building that had hosted five nights of Dire Straits at 12,000 people each, and was therefore already gearing up for huge audiences, it was decidedly underwhelming. Yet even despite this early naff effort, Biggar himself immediately realised that the sport had huge potential.

'We put everyone in a central block, right on the red line, we gave the team the big build up; the lights, the smoke, the nicknames, the whole works, and um, there was an odd atmosphere . . . but uh, *I* was hooked – from that game. It was fantastic. At the time I was still playing football, it was the first hockey game I'd ever seen, and I just couldn't believe it. "How the hell can they skate like that? How can they hit . . . and not get hurt?" The speed, the ferocity, the general mayhem that encompassed the whole game – I just sat there gobsmacked. I had a radio in my hand and I don't think I listened to it all night, I just sat there spellbound, thinking "This is fantastic. What a game!"'

Despite the paucity of that inaugural crowd, the attendances quickly improved – a more concerted ticket giveaway resulted in a much healthier crowd of 2,750 for the second game, and things quickly started to build from there. With a constant diet of Mexican Waves, hand jives and a steady stream of Queen and

Snap records, those who came to the early games certainly enjoyed themselves. 'I have not been so excited by entertainment since the Beatles concerts more than 30 years ago,' Steelers' fan John Moralee was quoted as saying at the time. Unsurprisingly, the media quickly dubbed the whole thing Steelermania. By November the team was pulling in around 5,500 people – a staggering statistic when you think they were playing in the English league, which, at the time, was effectively hockey's third division. Surely, it couldn't last.

'I mean at this stage we were still giving away about 1,000 tickets per game,' recalls Biggar, 'but when was the bubble going to burst? We thought the bubble would burst once we took the free tickets away, but it didn't, they came back for more. It's always a judgement call. When do you stop complimentary tickets? We decided at Christmas "Right, that's it. Let's cut it right down. If people are going to come to the game then they are going to have to come on their own merits rather than just be handed a free ticket." And they came, they still turned up. There was a slight dip, we lost about one to one-and-a-half thousand, which caused one or two panics, but the box office quadrupled, and we had that solid foundation there on which to build.'

By season's end, the Steelers had broken new ground in British ice hockey. They had successfully launched the sport on an unsuspecting public and in their debut season they had not only averaged twice as many fans as the next best supported team – Premier Division Nottingham Panthers – they had also shattered the British attendance record several times with crowds topping 9,000 at season's end. If it all seems like it was an elegantly thought out strategy of Rommel-like ingenuity to bring booming crowds to games, the truth of the matter was that the Steelers were really just making it up as they went along, week by week. 'It was literally that,' concedes Biggar. 'Every Monday I'd sit down with the Steelers and say "What are we going to do this week?" We'd literally write the game programme, say "What music are we going to play?" – "I dunno, what CDs have you got?" It was that kind of format. We had a budget of zero, that first year. We begged, borrowed, cajoled, beat up and basically blackmailed everyone to give us anything that they could. It was like, "Do we really need to spend £400 on a newspaper advert?" "We've got to, to see if it works . . ." and it was literally done on a week-by-week basis. There was no strategy – because none of us had ever done a hockey game before.

'We managed to find some money, about £6,000, because of the gate money, and we went out with a short, sharp, advertising campaign – something on the radio, something in the papers, to see what kind of a reaction we could provoke. How do you promote this to a football-mad city like Sheffield? There was just Wednesday and United and there was no way we had a clue as to what we were doing. We were sending the guys around schools. We wrote to all the schools in Sheffield and said, "Bring the kids, see the Arena, sit down, experience the whole thing." And we did all that, and at the end of it, invariably Ron Shudra would appear, in full battle dress, six feet six inches in his skates, towering over these kids, and the kids would go "Wow." Ron's a good-looking guy, great with the patter, great with the kids – perfect front man, and he looked massive. We'd give each of the kids a free ticket and say "Go home, tell mum and dad about the Arena, and show them the free ticket." Now, you try telling a seven-year-old, who's had a walk around the Arena, met a giant, and who's got a free ticket, that he can't go to the game on Saturday and watch the giant play – it's an impossibility! We'd get parents phoning up saying, "Can I have another free ticket?" We'd say "No, sorry, you'll have to buy one – but we'll give you a good rate." Some of them got annoyed, saying, "You shouldn't do this with children, it's like giving them sweets, and we have to wean them off." We'd say, "It's a free ticket, you don't have to come." But they had no choice . . . (Smiles)

'And you see them there; the parents who had been dragged along by their kids, looking all glum, with their pint of beer, thinking (sarcastically) "Oh great. We're going to see a hockey game . . ." But after ten minutes they'd start to move, start to party, cheer up a little bit, and by the end of the first period they'd be "Woo-wooing" along with everyone else. And that was the first piece of the strategy. We thought, "Great. We know how to get to the kids. Now, how do we get to the football crowds?" We took the players to football games, walked them around the pitch with the mascot, brought the football teams to the ice hockey games, put them in the suites, made a big thing out of the likes of Chris Waddle, Dave Bassett etc, and all of a sudden we'd start to see Wednesday supporters jump on the Metrolink after football games and come down to the arena. At that stage we thought it would give them something to do. Either on a Friday night, after the match on a Saturday when they were still pumped up, or a Sunday night. Sheffield, I think at that time, was the fifth biggest city in the country, but there still wasn't an awful lot of people. We didn't have any money to go after anyone else, or any glamorous marketing plans, so we thought we'd go after sporting celebs and the football crowds. It was like when we had Cantona here (Manchester). We put him on the big screen and all the United fans thought "If it's good enough for him then it's good enough for me." And that was the policy we had at Sheffield.'

Another policy they had at Sheffield was unleashing announcer Dave Simms on the hockey world. Initially, it had been the job of two radio DJs from Hallam FM to present the Steelers matches, but something about them hadn't been quite right. 'They were awful,' is Biggar's assessment. 'They were radio DJs, no disrespect to them, they were extremely good on the airwaves, but they were lousy when it came to an ice hockey game. They didn't know one end of a stick from the other – but then again neither did anyone in the building.' The call went up for someone else to take up the reigns, they tried another announcer who was 'very much in the normal mode of a hockey presenter', but that didn't seem to work out either, and in desperation they turned to Simms. For Biggar, it was the turning point.

'We said "This is what we want you to do, this is what we want you to say, how to get the whole thing working." But there was no actual script. At that stage we still didn't know how to write a script for a hockey game. It was all very much fly by the seat of your pants – although as far as the public were concerned it was a precision instrument.' This 'precision instrument' basically involved Simms winding up the opposition mercilessly, cranking the crowd up as far as they would go, and creating an environment that was as entertaining for the home fans as it was hostile for the visiting ones. 'Simmsy brought a whole new attitude. But his attitude matched that of the team. Simmsy was arrogant, cocksure, didn't give a damn about anything, knew zero about ice hockey, but "here we go". And he fitted the mould perfectly from the Steelers perspective.'

Indeed, he did. To an extent, Simms's attitude came to define the Sheffield Steelers, particularly where fans of the other teams were concerned. 'By that stage it was Simmsy on a leash,' recalls Biggar, 'but the leash was now about 300 yards long. He came out of the kennel, and he wasn't biting other teams' ankles, he was just going in and tearing other teams' heads off. Would we have had him again? I think so, he was the right man at the right time for the right job. I still think he's good now. He's still berated. He's now only the second best commentator in hockey circles, (laughs) Jon Hammond has obviously taken his crown, easily. But, I wouldn't have changed anything, we had a bloody good time, we made an awful lot of mistakes, we got an awful lot right – as the record books will show – but there's nothing you would change. It was a case of "We don't care, we're the Sheffield Steelers. We're the biggest thing in ice hockey since sliced bread. We've got massive crowds. We're hugely arrogant. We're over the top. If you don't like it – tough. 'Cos we are it. Full stop. End of story."' And of course, plenty of people didn't like it.

'There was huge resentment throughout hockey circles,' remembers Biggar. This came not only from the fans of the other clubs, who, obviously, were hardly likely to welcome this cocky new club with open arms, but perhaps surprisingly, also from the BIHA – at least in the early days. Whilst it seems amazing now that a club could arrive on the scene with facilities like Sheffield and be asked to enter the league at the lowest level and play teams who could only draw a few hundred to games in their own buildings, that's exactly what happened to the Steelers. 'We had wanted to start off in what was then the Premier Division, and the BIHA said "No. You're not allowed to,"' explains Biggar. 'We then tried to buy the Solihull Barons, but we were told "No, you can't." Everyone in the country said, "You will start, as everyone else has, at the bottom." So we started at the bottom and worked our way up.' Whilst this meant that for two seasons the Premiership sides were looking over their shoulder in much the same way a Reliant Robin driver will anxiously keep checking his rear view mirror as he hears a juggernaut bearing down on him, it did at least allow the Steelers to rear their supporters on a diet of steady victories, which Biggar admits was a big help in building up a following.

'No-one supports a loser – apart from Man City fans – but, to start with, you've got to have a winning team. People have said we were lucky in that Sheffield were the winning team. What would have happened if they'd been stuffed by every team on the planet? It would have been an awful lot harder, there's no disguising the fact. Everybody loves a winning team. But having said that, last year (1996/97) here at the Storm we ended up seventh out of eight and attendances were up by 28.1 per cent! You've got to win at the *start* though. The Steelers were virtually an impregnable fortress at home, the majority of the fans would only ever see the team win, and wouldn't be interested in the away games.'

Despite their popularity in their own backyard the Steelers were reviled by other hockey fans – although the big-spending newcomers hardly set about the best way of endearing themselves to other clubs when they broke the wage-capping limit and stacked their roster with other teams' star players. Yet this hostility couldn't be explained by simple envy – there was more to it than that. Yes, the Steelers were a successful outfit who were seen to have bought their way to glory, but so too had the Cardiff Devils and Durham Wasps before them. Whilst both these sides had obviously been disliked by other clubs at the time, they never attracted the same level of animosity that the Steelers were now attracting. It wasn't so much the level of success the Steelers enjoyed that irked the old order, but the *manner* of their success. Yes, they were arrogant. Yes, they gloated unbearably when they won. But there was something else. An uneasy feeling that they weren't *really* hockey people. They didn't really belong to the sport. Whether or not this belief was correct – and although it's understandable, I don't think it is – it is easy to see how it might have developed.

Whilst it's obviously a generalisation, to an extent the people who supported Fife, Nottingham or Cardiff etc, were hockey fans first and foremost, whilst the Sheffield supporters were *Steelers* fans first. At other clubs, the typical hockey fan would not only follow the British game, but also North America's National Hockey League (NHL), the pinnacle of the sport at club level, so you'd often be as likely to see Boston Bruins or Toronto Maple Leafs shirts in the crowd as you would the sweater of the home team. At Sheffield they barely knew the outside hockey world existed. Why would they? Their introduction to the sport was to see a dominant team playing out of a facility light years ahead of its rivals. Naturally, a degree of arrogance would creep in. With Simms urging the team and the crowd on, whilst decrying the opposition every step of the way, it's no surprise that the Steelers fans looked down on everyone else. It was the way they were brought up. Normal hockey protocol simply didn't apply to them, to the obvious chagrin of the rest of the sport.

This manifested itself most obviously one year at the Wembley Championships, an event when, traditionally, thousands of hockey fans from all over Britain would make the pilgrimage to London to indulge themselves in a weekend-long orgy of hockey, hockey, beer and more hockey – regardless, sometimes, of whether or not their team had actually made it to the finals. The weekend finals were legendary for the camaraderie and bonhomie amongst supporters. The great hockey party. In 1994, in what was still only their third season, the Sheffield Steelers unleashed themselves upon Wembley for the first time, bringing their supporters with them in far greater numbers than had been seen before from just one club. They seemed to take the place over. They were good-humoured, boisterous, noisy, they got fully behind their team, and they sang their hearts out regardless of the scorelines. Needless to say, everyone else hated them. The party had been rudely gatecrashed. When the Cardiff Devils took the Steelers apart 12–1 in the final it seemed to be like the old order reminding the upstarts that they had a way to go yet, but at the same time everyone knew that things would never be quite the same again.

'I hate to say it, but the Steelers ruined Wembley,' one stall trader told me, when I asked him what he thought about the arrival of big arena teams on the British game. This surprised me. Surely, all these extra people coming to the game had to be good for the hockey industry in this country. 'Well, I used to sell much more in the years before they arrived. They don't care about other teams, or the NHL, they're only interested in the Steelers. If I'm selling trading cards, they don't want to buy Gretzky or Lemieux, they just ask me if I have Ken Priestlay or Steve Nemeth – they don't understand that in the States these guys were nobodies, no one is interested.'

Of course, this wasn't the first time this had happened in British hockey. Years before, the fans of Cardiff had gone through a similar learning curve when their team quickly rose up through the ranks and became a dominant force. They too had been resented, but over time they had been accepted into the fold, as the rest of hockey had absorbed them and as they, themselves, had acquired a greater appreciation of the game. For the Steelers it was different. Their sheer weight of numbers just seemed overwhelming to other supporters. Rather than being seen as newcomers to the game, to be welcomed by the rest of the community, they simply appeared as a huge threat. Of course many of these feelings would dissipate in time (except in Nottingham, obviously) as the Steelers fans became more hockey literate, only for a similar situation to arise when the Manchester Storm started to build up momentum and once again the sport was flooded with thousands of new fans who didn't know what they were talking about, and would have been wise to remember that a closed mouth gathers no feet. Within a few months of the Manchester Storm first taking to the ice the *Ice Hockey News Review* was quickly awash with letters, either from opinionated Storm fans who were happy to set the world to rights, or from all the other fans who could barely contain their glee at putting the boot into the naive newcomers. Ironically, as the wheel turned full circle, some of this vitriol came from Steelers fans. 'It's great listening to some of the Steelers fans now,' says Biggar, 'either some of them forget, on purpose, or some of them weren't around when the team were going through down spots. The Steelers fans now think that they know everything there is to know about the game; that they know every rule and regulation, and they are really impatient with some of the other newcomers, but it's a short memory. On the fan appreciation side [in the early days], well they didn't know an awful lot. It was just fun. Who knew the rules at Sheffield? Nobody had a clue.'

But there had been some casualties. Stewart Roberts, who has been compiling his excellent *Ice Hockey Annual* for 22 years, reported that this year (1997/98), despite the sport attracting far greater crowds at the top level than had ever been thought possible, his yearbook had sold less well than in previous years – suggesting that in some respects, whilst the sport had attracted plenty of new fans, they were not necessarily as devoted to the sport as some of the traditional fans. Furthermore, it seemed it was having an adverse effect on those old fans and making some of them less passionate about the sport. The new generation of hockey fans were flocking to the sport because it was becoming fashionable, which was great, but would they keep coming back? It was great that the Manchester Storm pulled in such massive crowds, but at the same time these crowds would fluctuate so wildly – a five-figure Superleague crowd one night would tumble to less than half that for a European game a few days later – that it suggested the bumper crowds were misleading. People were viewing ice hockey as entertainment first and foremost, rather than as a sport. Whilst this might not sound like it is a bad thing, it does suggest that the traditionally small, but loyal, following that the game had was being displaced by a larger, but more fickle audience. The age of the arena had arrived and the marketing men had done a great job in selling the game, but the only place some of the old fans thought they'd sold it was down the river; an accusation levelled at the Steelers all too often.

'Basically it was like "The Sheffield Steelers have ruined British ice hockey,"' replied Biggar when I asked him what kind of reaction they had got from other fans. 'I heard it so many times "Do you realise what you've done?" "Yeah, we've done 10,150 people, we're on TV, we're getting national press, we get people through the doors, we attract sponsorship, we're the biggest thing in Sheffield, so how have we ruined things?" "You've thrown the values out of the window." "No. We've created Entertainment with a capital E, take it or leave it, we've totally and utterly broken the mould." I had three great seasons with the Steelers. First year we came second, second year, second place, third year we got to Wembley, and got hammered 12–1 by Cardiff [laughs]. But this was a huge, huge success story. We did the 10,150 and said "That's it. Ice hockey is never ever going to get any bigger in this country. This is the peak. It is no longer a minority sport."'

Indeed the mould had been broken, but at the time there wasn't much sense that the Steelers were setting the trail for everyone else. 'At that stage it was really a case of "Who cares about anyone else? We're the Sheffield Steelers." That was the philosophy. It was "Make money. The team has to make money." It wasn't there as a loss leader, to be a nice, pretty addition to the Arena. It gave us a solid foundation from an arena operative's perspective with the community in Sheffield, which was really nice – you can't buy that kind of PR, but at the end of the day, it had to make money. It was only when Steve Crowther came in that all of a sudden it became this real, professional club, with budgets, departments, organisation and planning, and then it became a real hockey team and not just a collection of extras from *Slapshot*.

'Steelers lost money in the first year, lost in the second, lost in the third . . . George (Dodds, owner) will say that they lost in the fourth, fifth, sixth and seventh as well, but they had started to get it right at that stage. The weekly meetings were then just that, rather than having a meeting on the Monday, then two hours later "We need an idea", three hours later "We need another idea". I'd sit down with Clive Tuyl and Steve Crowther every Monday and we'd say "What do we need to do this week?" It was still done on a very short term, but at least we'd established the rules, regulations and campaign that we were going to follow throughout that particular season. We just modified it on a weekly basis. We made hundreds of mistakes, but we had it going in the right direction by then. A lot of the Steelers' credit always goes to Alex Dampier and Clive Tuyl, but without Steve Crowther that team wouldn't be here anymore. I know you've got George Dodds and George is brilliant, but it was Steve who steadied the ship, and said "This is how it's going to work. We're going to be a professional team, in a big arena and it's going to be a money-making team." And it had to be like that from day one, so it was a case of "Bollocks to the rest of British ice hockey. We don't care."'

But whether they cared or not, they *had* changed the landscape of the British game. With the Steelers outdrawing many local football clubs it was inevitable that they would catch the eye of others and wouldn't stay the only big fish in the pond for long. Even before Sheffield Arena had opened, plans were afoot for a building in Manchester with almost twice the capacity, and when this came online, Biggar, to his surprise, found himself having to repeat the Steelers' success story in another city. It had never been in his plans.

Ogden Entertainment Services, the American company that runs the Nynex arena, never planned to run an ice hockey team in Manchester. Running a sports team was a risky business, and after all, what did they know about it anyway? They were arena operatives, not sports people. Besides, they had had their fingers burned once before in Anaheim when they had tried to get an indoor soccer team playing out of the Arrowhead Pond – home of the Mighty Ducks, and it had just haemorrhaged money. They'd tried to sell football to an audience used to ice hockey and regretted it, so why would they want to try and sell ice hockey to an audience used to football? It just didn't make sense. However, since it had always been the plan for hockey to be played there, in 1995, as the building neared completion, Ogdens were still deep in negotiation with another American firm who were supposed to be organising that side of things. Dave Biggar, who by this stage had jumped arenas from Sheffeld to Manchester, takes up the story.

'We sat down with the Cook Group, who at that stage owned the franchise rights for both basketball and ice hockey in Manchester. They decided that they didn't want ice hockey. They were basketball people – always have been basketball people. So we bought the franchise off them, I think for a quid. We intended to then sell the franchise to someone who did want to do ice hockey. We approached some of the concert promoters who had expressed an interest in doing sports – Harvey Goldsmith had just bought into basketball, Barry Marshall, who does Tina Turner and Bryan Adams, had just gone into basketball as well. We couldn't find anyone who wanted to do it. So I sat down one day, worked out some figures, and said, "Why don't we run the team?" One of the reasons I had been brought over from Sheffield was because of the experience I had had with the Steelers. But Ogdens didn't know anything about running a team. I put together a budget, sat down with the American corporate chiefs and said "I reckon we can do this. We can put it together. Let's have a go."'

It's fair to say that Ogdens weren't exactly chomping at the bit. For one thing, who were they supposed to get to run this team? 'I said, "Simple, we have to get the best guy in the country in for the job." They said "Who is it?" I said "John Lawless."' At the time, it certainly did seem like Lawless was the man for the job. Still only 34, Lawless had enjoyed a remarkable career as a player at Peterborough and player-coach at Cardiff, where he had led the club to Grand Slam triumph and European glory. When it came to launching a new team in a new building, Lawless was clearly top dog. However, there was the slight complication that his Devils team were still busy fighting to resist the challenge of the ever improving Steelers. A year on from their Wembley debut, the Steelers had descended on London again, determined to win this time so as to add to their recently collected Premier Division title, and they were up against Cardiff in the semi-final. This didn't sound like the perfect time for Biggar to go tapping on Lawless's shoulder.

'We went down to Wembley. I sat down with Lee Esckilsen (Executive Director of the arena at the time) and he said "How are we going to do this?" I said "It's quite simple. If Cardiff lose, we go to the press conference, blag our way in, sit down with John and say 'Now that the team's lost, can we offer you a new challenge?' If they win, then we'll wait until the final tomorrow and if they lose that, we'll do the same. If they win *that*, then we might have to wait a little longer . . . "' Fortunately for Biggar, the Devils lost in the semi-finals after a rollercoaster match had ended in a dramatic penalty shot victory for the Steelers – who would go on to clinch the Championship the next day. As his players changed, Lawless made his way to the post-match press conference whilst Biggar and Esckilsen lurked in wait.

'We waited for him behind one of the doors. One of the press guys told John that someone wanted to talk to him, so he came out. I'd got one of the Manchester arena brochures in my jacket, folded, with pictures of the arena, all the reasons why he should come to Manchester. We told him what we wanted, and gave John the brochure. John laughs about this now, because the brochure was bright fluorescent green, A4 size, "Manchester arena" written all over the front, and John just had his normal coach's suit on and nowhere to put this damn brochure. He said "This is great, you've given me a fluorescent green piece of information with 'Manchester arena' written all over it. How am I going to walk back into the Cardiff dressing room with this?" So he just shoved it down the front of his trousers, buttoned his jacket up and stood there with this bulge . . . Bloody hell.

'He's only a little guy, but he just seemed to have put on platform shoes by the time we'd finished. It was obviously something he'd been interested in. He said, "You know, I'm with Cardiff now, I've signed a contract, I'll need time to think about it." He walked away and I said to Lee, "He's coming. His team's just been beaten by Sheffield, he's got nowhere else to go. Sheffield are on the ascendancy. He wants to get back, to be the biggest. He'll be here." And lo and behold, the little man came. And we had to set it all up again . . . '

With Biggar's Sheffield experience to draw upon, the marketing team sat down with Lawless, assistant Daryl Lipsey, and Cardiff player Shannon Hope (who at the time seemed set to join the club, only to later decide to stay put and concentrate on his Shine Dog clothing business in Wales) and started to map out their strategy. If they were going to do things right, and sell this new team to the public, then they were going to have to come up with a catchy name. Choosing one, however, was never going to be easy. 'The name was absolute agony,' recalls Biggar, obviously still scarred from the experience. 'Me, Lee Esckilsen – who's the world's most miserable, boring man, I have to put that on record – John Lawless and Shinedog (Shannon Hope) were in Grinch, the wine bar in town. We were all getting a little tipsy, we're thinking "What are we going to call this team?"'

Though Storm fans can sleep easily in their beds now, the frontrunner at the time was the Mighty Dogs of Manchester . . . 'Shannon had brought in this fabulous design, with a dog skull head in a goalie mask, with two bones crossed in the background, and "Mighty Dogs of Manchester" written on it,' Biggar recollects. It quickly grabbed their imaginations. 'We were going to call the building "The Kennel", the penalty boxes "The Dog Pound". We were going to get everyone in the audience to bark . . . We sat there and got louder and louder. And Lee sat there getting more and more annoyed because he didn't like the name. He wanted to call it the "Manchester Rockets", because he reckoned the first steam train had come out of Manchester and was called the Rocket – I thought it had

come from Newcastle, but he was convinced it was Manchester.'
(In the interests of journalistic research, I tried to find out if
Esckilsen had been right on the origin of Stephenson's Rocket. I
discovered that it was indeed built for the Liverpool–Manchester
line, but couldn't find out *where* it was built. I would have
pursued this investigation further but I was afraid of being
drawn in to the murky and sordid world of the railway
enthusiast and, understandably, I recoiled. Sorry to let you
down.)

'Then John jumped up and said, "I know. We'll do some
audience research." Lee thought, "Okay, I can handle that.
When do you want to do it?" John said "Now!" and jumped up
towards this table full of girls, and said, "Hello, I'm John
Lawless. I'm going to run the ice hockey team in Manchester."
They said, "What's ice hockey?" We explained it was a game for
big, strong, powerful guys. They looked at him, and simply
refused to believe he was an ice hockey player. He went round
the tables saying, "What do you think of these names?" – we'd
all started barking at this stage, and we just went round the
whole bar, "What do you think of the name the Mighty Dogs of
Manchester?" getting people's reactions. We came back and
everyone had said "What a *crap* name!"

'Lee was smiling now, but we wouldn't give up. I ran back to
the office, I know the guy who's in charge of the Mighty Ducks
(the Disney-owned NHL team in Anaheim) and we rang him up
and said, "We're going to call our team the Mighty Dogs of
Manchester, any objections?" And he said, "Can you put it on a
fax?" So we faxed the logo over, and we got the answer back "If
you even so much as *think* of using the name we'll hammer you
for everything." They'd shown it to their solicitors. So we had
no choice.' With disaster thus narrowly averted, it was back to
square one. 'We came up with others, Manchester Lightning,
Manchester Rain, kept coming back to the Rockets. We all
thought the Rockets was a crap name. Lee thought it was a
brilliant name. He said we couldn't possibly call it Manchester
Storm, because it would upset the Greater Manchester Visitors
and Convention mob who were trying to get away from this

image of a rainy city. It would upset the Tampa Bay Lightning – 'cos at that stage we were talking about using their colours. "No. We are not going to call it the Storm, I want it to be called the Rockets."

'It kept going back and forth, back and forth amongst other, more important things – like opening the building. We'd got a £54 million building opening and we were worrying about what to call a bloody ice hockey team.' Indeed, time was pressing. Sooner or later, they were going to have to commit themselves to a name. The Storm was now a front runner, even though the name didn't scan very well – Biggar recalls at one meeting all these guys in suits trying out chants and moaning that a one syllable name was difficult to sing. Finally, at one of these regular board meetings, just before the building was due to open, they took the plunge. 'Myself, David Davies, and John Lawless said "Right, that's it. When they (the other directors) all come back in after lunch, we've decided. We're going to call it the Manchester Storm, because the Storm will always reign in Manchester."' And so the team, at last, had a name. Now they needed an announcer.

There was a rumour going round at the time that it might be a certain Mr Simms, but as it turned out, Biggar had someone else pencilled in for the job. 'I'd already got hold of Jon Hammond, who I'd known since 1986, and said, "Jon, I've got a great one for you – ice hockey." He just looked at me and said, "What on earth is ice hockey?" So I took him to a Steelers game, he said, "Okay, I understand. But you don't want me to be like *him* do you?" I said, "No, I want you to be Jon Hammond." I've worked with Jon on a million and one things, from royal fashion shows to major concerts, and he's the best. End of story. No negotiation. I think Jon was the first person we signed for the Storm. He'll hate me for saying this, but Jon said "I can't do this. I'm a professional."'

If Hammond thought he was going to be asked to repeat Simms's style, he was mistaken. Whilst that approach had worked well for Sheffield, Biggar wasn't so sure it would be helpful at Manchester. 'At Sheffield it was aggressive. It was antagonistic. It was in your face, belittle the opposition when they come into the building, have a real go. For three years whilst I was at the Steelers, and even now, the Steelers are vilified throughout the rest of British hockey. It's great for Sheffield, but I didn't think it would be as good for Manchester. It's a bigger city. With due respect to everyone in Sheffield, it's a bit more cosmopolitan, it's a little bit more cultured. How do we get the same kind of reaction from the punters but not be as aggressive?'

Lawless, too, thought it needed something different. 'I know some announcers are biased, but that guy goes too far,' he told me that summer. You could see what he meant. The trouble with the Simms approach is that it winds up the opposition. That's okay if you can be sure of beating them, but in a close encounter it can give them an edge. In the inaugural Superleague season it was evident that other teams relished beating the Steelers more than any other side, even Cardiff who were the better side at the time, and nothing got supporters going more than seeing the Sheffield side lose. Over the course of the season, when the Steelers were struggling for form, it may even have been the factor that tipped some games away from them, and only helped Cardiff as they took the title. Lawless didn't want an announcer to do anything to incite the opposition, and was careful to vet the match programme on a number of occasions to remove anything that might inflame the visitors. Whilst this censorship was criticised in some quarters, my own feeling is that Lawless was spot-on. When the Storm started up it was obvious that they would attract a similar level of resentment from other teams that the Steelers had. With this in mind, a softer approach to game night presentation seemed to make sense.

Biggar agreed. 'We sat with Jon and said "How do you want to play this? We don't want the crowd to side with the opposition, and we don't want them to totally harangue the opposition – but at the end of the day it's still the Storm's building. Let's go for a more even approach, a more even atmosphere, but still generate the excitement we need to put on a game." We did get that balance.' To this end, the Hammond approach was a more subtle affair than the old gung-ho Steelers approach, with the home crowd discouraged from booing visiting teams, and a more genial, family atmosphere encouraged. There was also a considerable shift in emphasis towards the role of the scoreboard which, unlike at other rinks, did considerably more than just tell you the score and how long was left to play.

At the Nynex, the scoreboard was a monster, a million pound four-screened behemoth that was able to show live action and replays in full colour, and run a constant stream of film clips and adverts to keep the audience entertained. For Biggar, its importance cannot be underestimated. 'Today's public is a TV public. They drink, smoke and eat TV. This is perfect for them. A Storm game is a live event and a television production at the same time. One of the punters said to me, "It's brilliant. It's like watching a live event in your own living room, where you've got the pause button so you can go out and get something to eat or drink from the kitchen and you come back and you've not missed anything. You've got the action replays, the ads that come on, interference from the kids so that you want to turn the volume up – it's just unbelievable that you've managed to combine a live event with TV production at the same time. It just makes us all feel at home." And that's what I wanted from the start. Lets make this a total NHL ice hockey production – though having said that, we've had people in from the NHL who've said "This is unbelievable. We don't do it to this extent." But it had to be different from the Steelers, 'cos everyone would have just said "Biggar. He's done this with the Steelers, he'll do exactly the same in Manchester." And we didn't. We'd learnt from the Steelers.'

The Steelers' scoreboard, which looked pretty good before the Storm arrived on the scene, suddenly looked rather ordinary now that the Nynex had opened its doors. Storm fans were quick to dub it 'The Gameboy'. 'I wouldn't go so far as to say it was the Steelers' downfall, but it was a major *faux pas* in terms of the marketing and promotion of the game, though that's easy to say in hindsight,' concedes Biggar. 'It was available at the time, but SMG (the arena's operatives) took the decision to go with the simple two colour dot matrix, and perhaps the Steelers should have said they'd help upgrade it, whatever. That was a mistake made on both sides that they regret now, and will continue to regret for a while. It's like a bad reception from Channel 5. It would make a big difference to Sheffield, it would bring them back to within . . . six warp factors of us.

'The biggest advice I could give to the new Leeds team, if it's a choice of marble on the concourse floor, at the cost of, whatever million, and sticking a screen up – stick the screen up. I don't care whatever else they do in the building – it could be gilt edged, shag-pile carpet, a chauffeur-driven limo for every member of the audience, it would mean nothing unless you've got that screen. Do not even contemplate not having a screen in that building. If it costs four or five million, make it the first cheque you sign. It's massively important.'

So armed with a scoreboard that cost more to assemble than any of the teams they played, the Storm set about winning over the punters of Manchester. After the dismal opening night at Sheffield, Biggar was much better prepared for the opener in Manchester, which drew a highly impressive 10,034 – although having said that, a considerable portion of the audience was made up of contingents from Cardiff, who were there to wish Lawless luck, and Sheffield, who were presumably so guilt-ridden about missing their own opener they felt they needed to make amends with the new building.

By the end of the Storm's first season, they were second only to the Steelers in terms of crowd support, averaging over 7,000 a game in the league and breaking the British attendance record three times along the way. It was way above Biggar's expectations. 'The projection in the first year was 3,000 by Christmas, 4,000 during the second half and 5,000 for the play-offs. That would have been enough to satisfy our elders back in the States.' In fact, they twice drew over 16,000, and on the first occasion it happened, when 16,280 saw them collect the Division One trophy against local rivals Blackburn in February

1996, it sent shock waves rippling across the Pond. That same night, seven games were played in the NHL. The Storm crowd beat six of them. Ogdens were well chuffed.

In the second season, despite the team's stubborn refusal to actually be any good, the Storm overtook Sheffield as the country's best supported team. The icing on the cake came in the final game of the regular season when, with the help of local TV and a large contingent of Sheffield fans, the Storm filled the Nynex for the first time (except for the 26 seats that Sky took up). The crowd of 17,245 was all the more amazing when you think that they had to turn over 2,000 home fans away. For Biggar, it showed the potential of the sport. 'There's no reason why we can't do 17,000 for every game, there isn't enough entertainment out there where people can sit down as a family, have a bloody good time, where students can come in cheaply, and then go on to a club after. We could be the Manchester United of European ice hockey. We've only got 17,500 seats to fill – there's 11,000,000 people out there. It's not a bad ratio when you think about it.'

With all these people pouring through the doors, the obvious conclusion to arrive at is that someone, somewhere, is making a tidy little sum out of the Storm. However, as Biggar is careful to explain, the economics of the team are a complex old affair. 'It costs in excess of a million pounds to run this team, not even for a year, just for the season. The way it works is that the Storm are treated as a separate entity from the rest of the building. The Storm rent the Nynex Arena Manchester from Ogden Entertainment.' On favourable terms, presumably? 'No. They rent it at the current rate. We actually said "If we are going to run this ice hockey team, what is the real, real cost of running an ice hockey team?" Not, "Oh we'll only charge you £5,000 for the building." What is the real cost of running a hockey team from start to finish?' Erm, quite a lot, I imagine.

'The staff time that is allocated to the Storm is taken into account – 75 per cent of Jo's (Jo Houlcroft, marketing) time is taken up with the hockey, so 75 per cent of her salary goes into it, 40 per cent of my time is with the Storm, so that goes against the Storm's budget etc. It's got its own marketing budget, vehicle, insurance, public liability and the rental. The building gets the rental from the Storm, money back from the beverages and a percentage of all the merchandise sold. It all goes back into the same pot at the end of the day, but there's no favouritism given at all. Because of the complexity of running the chiller pads, maintaining everything that we need – the dasher boards and the plexi-glass – the Storm end up paying more than the Manchester Giants (Cook's basketball team) do. The refrigeration process has to be paid for by the Storm. So it's a case of, strip away everything, take the ice away, take the plexi-glass away, how much would we save by not having the Manchester Storm? And how much do we make by having the Storm in the building? So in all, the team costs easily in excess of £1 million to run. We don't get that back on ticket sales.' This is bad news. Those of us who have been planning to win the lottery and buy our own team are going to have to think again. To run a hockey team at this level now, means you'll have to win it on a rollover week.

'The team itself, and its costs, are effectively met by the audience coming through the doors. But then there's the admin side, and everything else. Once you add in sponsorship, signage, programme sales, merchandise; then that's where we build up most of the shortfall. So if people say "Well, all of these people, surely that's enough to pay for the team." Yeah. Easily enough to pay for the team, by £10,000. The team is paid for by you lot attending. Now, if you want them to play on ice . . . If you want the scoreboard switched on – every time we switch the scoreboard on it costs us a grand. There's a 12 man crew just to run the scoreboard. The producer gets paid . . . an awful lot of money, then there's the cameramen. There's ten people in Graham Nurse's (matchnight co-ordinator) lot, backstage and in the changing room area. Then you've got all the bar staff, the security, it's a costly old affair – but it's worth it. Without it, the building would lose money, whereas with it, the building is in a profit ratio.' Music to Ogden's ears, presumably.

'The Storm can lose money as long as the arena makes

money,' Biggar explains. 'Ogden's won't do anything unless it makes them money.' Simple as that. Richard Ablon (the worldwide president of Ogden's, the man in the big chair, with power of death over every Ogden employee) was in London in January 1997. He happened to pick up the sports pages and saw that the Storm had got stuffed by Cardiff, (3–11 at home, a performance even more lamentable than it sounds, as I recall . . .) read that, got hold of America immediately, and said "Find out what the team needs. Ogden's need a winning team. If they need more money to get more players, give them more money to get more players." Though we still have to make a profit at the end of the year. They constantly stick us under the microscope.

'When the NHL reported that a British team called the Manchester Storm had beaten six out of seven teams in the States in attendances, the NHL started to talk to Ogden about the Manchester Storm. Our chief can pick up the phone and talk to Gary Bettman (NHL commissioner). The NHL are starting to talk about us. Ogdens now use us as an example of how they can take a blank piece of paper and turn it into this huge money-making venture, crowd pleaser and enormous community PR programme with sponsorship and everything else attached to it. And that for them is massively important as a tool throughout the rest of the world. They've used that as a basis for some of the presentations they've done in Europe, and some of the presentations they've done in the States. "Oh, do you realise we've got a hockey team in England?" Everyone in America bursts out laughing, then they say, "Yeah, they actually drew 17,240 people . . . " It's acutely important for them, but at the end of the day they've got to make money.

'It's a five-year plan. We lost money in the first season, we lost money in the second season, although we lost less. This year the plan is to again lose money, but only a little bit, break even the year after that, and then move into profit. If we can get ahead of that, fine. But now it's gone from being "Oh, just get on with it," to being hugely important to the building. Food, beverage, merchandising, the community side – you can measure what the Storm do for us in terms of crisps sales, etc, but in terms of community relations it has been of intangible benefit that you just couldn't put a value on. When we first did audience research in 16 towns throughout the region, the game had a two per cent interest in the region. After last year it was up to 17 per cent and 22 per cent in some areas. In terms of our local catchment area the Storm have saved us hundreds of thousands of pounds in terms of advertising and marketing costs. My marketing budget has gone down massively just because of the Storm.'

With the sound of all these cash tills ringing, it's no surprise that other parties started to sniff around the team. 'After the first year we got a lot of offers to sell the team. But we thought – why? We have total control here. We're control freaks. Total control freaks in this building. Now it's a case of, "Sorry, the team is not for sale." We don't want a partnership, we will continue to own the team, we will run it through its five-year plan and then decide what to do with it. Do we sell it? Do we keep it? I'm saving my pocket money,' laughs Biggar. Aha, I thought. The man's already started scheming. 'Basically, if you see crowds drop to 4,000 a game, and the game presentation's crap then you can think – hang on, Biggar's doing this on purpose! I've never wanted to own anything in my life, but you look at this and think – why should we give this away?'

As the Storm crowds had risen in number, they'd also risen in awareness. As had happened at Sheffield before, some of them even started to learn the rules. This hadn't always been the case – I fondly recall Cardiff getting a delayed call in that 11–3 game when they were already well ahead, and pulling their netminder for the extra skater. A guy behind me, not picking up on the subtlety of the move, moaned 'Bloody hell, look at that. They're taking the piss now.' Of course, as the crowd got more into the swing of the game Biggar found that he didn't need to hold their hands so often. Although they still had a way to go – they had an annoying tendency to start Mexican waves at key points in the game, they were slowly becoming more, dare I say it, sophisticated. 'I think it started to happen during the second half of last season (the 2nd). You'd see them becoming critical of plays, so what we did on the music side was, back off. Take the volumes down. In some instances don't play any music during the breaks to see what happens to the audience, and the audience by that stage have got their own momentum. They know what is happening.'

Part of the reason for this wasn't just because they were getting used to the game, it was also because the demographics of the audience were changing. 'We used to have, in that first season, a 60/40 kids majority audience. Second season we got it down to 51 per cent adults. There's still an awful lot of kids in the audience – Sheffield is something like 68 per cent adults. This year, with season tickets, we've got 67 per cent adults.' Whilst this statistic is good news for the die-hard fans who found match nights often more like a crèche than a hockey audience, and who longed for a 'serious' crowd at the Nynex – or people like me, who simply hate children – Biggar is still pleased to see so many young faces in the support. 'The kids, we need them. They are the toughest audience to get, but they are the adults of the future, so let's try and keep the kids.'

Of course, and it's very easy to forget amongst the glitz and razzamatazz, another reason that people come in their thousands to watch Sheffield or Manchester is because they like the players. Traditionally, hockey did very well as a grassroots sport. You would go to the rink, watch local lads smash each other's teeth out, see the odd flashy import, and then head to the bar and get drunk with all of them. Now, as the game becomes more and more professional, the local lad is something of a rarity, and what would once have been a squad with say three imports, is now a squad with three Brits if you're lucky. At the start of the 1997/98 Superleague season for instance, less than 15 per cent of the squads was made up of British players. From a marketing point of view, whilst by no means an insurmountable problem, it is a bit of a drawback.

'The public like the American and Canadian accents because it adds that showbiz extra. But if there was someone in there who was a good looking British boy, who looked right, sounded right, could play properly, it would be fantastic.' Admits Biggar, 'Everyone goes on to me about Cardiff and Stevie Lyle. Brilliant. Phenomenal. What was he, 14 when he first played in goal for them? 17 years old, great netminder, he's with an NHL farm team. Brilliant. Fabulous. But he's a netminder, you can't see him! Give me Rob Lowe, with a body like one of the Gladiators, who can beat the hell out of everyone, who can score goals, who can skate as fast as hell *and* can talk to the media with a Manchester accent – he would be sent from heaven. Brilliant. That's what it needs.' Despite the temptation to quote him out of context on wanting Rob Lowe with a great body, I can't help but agree with him. Hockey has come a long way in the last few years, but what it needs is a homegrown player to become a household name.

'We tended to do it with "Local Hero" Nick Crawley and Alan "Hollywood" Hough, but you can only take it so far. If there was a guy out there . . . I mean, everyone said Nicky Chinn or David Longhurst. Nicky Chinn ain't good looking enough. Good ice . . . bloody *great* ice hockey player, but he's not a good looking boy. David Longhurst, another great player, not a good enough looking boy. Stephen Cooper, good looking boy . . . but he's a bit shy. And he's a defenceman. We need our own Great One – a Great Britain One. But if you could get someone like that, then that's it, you know – strap him down, tie him to a management contract, register his name, register his nickname, register everything and turn him into the Cantona . . . the *British* Cantona, of ice hockey and you'd have one hell of a field day. Britain needs someone like that. It would really fire the imagination.

'Everyone had a go at us for getting rid of Hough, (Tim) Dempsey and Nick, but they weren't good enough. Simple as that. It's a horrible fact, but they just weren't good enough to play with the big boys. If there are kids out there that can, it would be our dream. Say after five years, I don't know, a kid who started watching the Storm at 12, he's already started figure skating, he then comes to the Storm matches and in five years time we pick him up as a rookie 17- or 18- year old. That would be a hell of a prospect.' For the time being, though, Biggar would just have to work with the players he had. In the first two years of the Storm, probably the most popular crowd favourite was, ironically considering his position, American netminder John 'Vegas' Finnie.

'The media loved him. The crowds loved him. He was relaxed, he was a character. He could talk, he could make the spectacular save – he'd let in some *crap* goals, but it was a case of it's Finnie! We came up with the "Viva Las Vegas" thing because he was known to visit a casino every now and then – when he was awake – and the Vegas thing took off. He was an ideal marketing dream. If he comes back this season away we go again, if he doesn't (he didn't) then we've got to turn someone else into a hero.' And this, despite what individual players may like to think about themselves from time to time, is the stark reality. None of them is ever as indispensable as they may care to think. When the Storm sacked John Lawless, on orders from Ogden's American chiefs after a poor season, replacement Kurt Kleinendorst wanted to know where he stood with regards to the crowds' favourite players.

'When Kurt came in he asked "What happens if I don't sign *any* of last year's team? Forget the playing ability, but none of them come back? What happens if the fans' favourites, the supporters' player of the year etc, don't come back? What are you going to do?"' remembers Biggar. It wasn't a question he had particularly wanted to hear, but the answer was fairly straightforward. 'Well, we turned them into fan favourites, we gave them the nicknames, we wound the crowd up with them, we added the music, we gave them the profiles. If you take them away from us all that means is that we'll have to turn them round again. But, if you take away a netminder who is the most popular netminder in the country, replace him with a netminder who is a better netminder than him. We're not going to say "His character's gotta be like this . . . ," or "He's gotta look like the following . . . " Make sure he's the best there is and people will forget who the other netminder was. If you're going to take a popular forward away, then give us a forward who scores goals like a machine, and he will soon turn into a fans' favourite. People forget easily – though saying that, they have a long memory. They forget if you give them what they want, but they have an awful long memory if you give them crap back as a replacement.'

In the event, for the Storm's third season, Biggar had to contend with 12 new players from a squad of 19. 'I sat down with Kurt and said "This player that you've signed, what's he like?" and Kurt said "He's got great hands, he can skate well, he can stop on a sixpence, he scores goals . . . " "What does he look like?" "Does it matter?" I said, "Well, you've signed him now . . . can he talk, has he got a nickname?" "How do you work this?" he wanted to know. I told him "You've signed him on his playing merits, fine. I don't care if he's got four eyes on the playing side, but once you've signed him give us something to play with. Give me something to work with. How tall is he? Give me photos, lets have some action shots."'

As I concluded my interview with Biggar, some details on a new signing, Stefan Ketola, came in. Immediately, Biggar started to look for an angle on how to sell the guy ('The bad boy of Swedish hockey'? Hmm, Cantona angle. 'Ooh ahh, Ke – to – la . . . ') and how his new teammates might need to be presented too. 'It's going to be hard, I mean, we built them up, we turned them into heroes with the fans' help, and now we've got new players in and we have to start again.' Indeed he did. All those seats weren't going to fill themselves . . .

The Brit Puck

Obviously, I love hockey. That goes without saying. (Or it would have done, had I not just said it then.) And I love going to games. But when you go to as many games as I do, going to hockey stops being this exotic, momentous event, and starts becoming routine. When you first fall in love with hockey, you want to see it all the time. You can't stop thinking about it. After the first few games you start to get curious, and decide that you want to watch it in other arenas too. You decide that maybe the time has come to stop watching other sports and settle down with this one. Pretty soon, it has taken your life over, and has begun to dominate your every waking thought. (I once got up at an obscenely early hour just to watch an episode of *Pingu* because I'd heard it was the episode where he plays hockey with his chums. It wasn't.) But, gradually, even though it is always very enjoyable, the glitter starts to fade, and what was once new and exciting has now become familiar and reassuring. Still nice. But not the same as it used to be.

This is why I like to take people along to games who have never been before, to vicariously see the game afresh and remind myself why it has the hold on me that it does. To see the way their eyes widen when they step into the arena and see the vast sweep of spectators spilling out before them. ('Gosh, I never knew so many people watched it . . . ') To sit back and wait for them to pick up on the energy of the crowd. ('Wow, it's a really good atmosphere . . . ') To see their faces once the game begins, and they have become mesmerised by the speed and explosive power of the skating. ('Fast, isn't it?') And like a kindly uncle indulging his inquisitive nephew at his first football game, I will field their stupid questions as they try to work out what the game is about, knowing that each answer I give will bring them closer and closer to being hooked. Often, their questions are easy to answer, and even if I don't really know the answer myself ('So why was that a coincidental penalty?') I can usually bluff my way through without too much discomfort. However, there is one question that I'm always uneasy about fielding, and no amount of stalling is going to cover up the sad truth.

'So, are all the players American, then?' My guest will venture, like a sceptical child inquiring about Father Christmas.

'No. Of course not . . . ' I respond, as though such a thing obviously would be terrible. 'They're Canadian,' I say. As if this makes any difference.

'What, *all* of them?'

'No, not *all* of them. Erm, some of them are from America, but the rest are Europeans . . . ' I say, hoping that the word 'Europeans' will make them think 'Britons'. It never does.

'So how many players are *British*, then?' they ask, turning around and looking at me suspiciously. I will tell them. If I'm lucky, I can point to three or four. Sometimes there aren't any at all.

'Oh,' they reply, and turn back to watch the game. It doesn't seem like it matters – after all, they still enjoy the game, but it does. I can tell they feel a bit cheated. A little let down. They were under the impression that they were watching a game of British ice hockey, when in fact all they were doing was watching a game of ice hockey in Britain. It's the only downside to the evening, but it hangs over me for the rest of the game.

To my eternal shame, I'd almost convinced myself that it really doesn't matter if all the Superleague players are imports. After a while, you kind of get used to it. The names that seemed alien and strange at first start to slide off your tongue, Montanari, Nienhuis, Herlofsky, Jablonski, and it doesn't seem that odd anymore. You can talk freely about the Ayr Scottish Eagles without blushing, even though you know their team are about as Scottish as Ayers Rock. You get to know the players, and, unaccountably, when you talk to them you start to use words like 'sophomore', and 'rookie'. You get used to saying 'schedules' instead of 'fixtures' and 'feisty' instead of 'niggly'. Although I've always drawn the line at speaking with a Canadian accent, I'm so used to hearing it now I hardly notice it any more. And then I got a jolt. The other day I spoke to a guy who plays in the Superleague and he had this weird accent. A guy called Ian Cooper. One of the highest scoring players in British hockey history. A guy from Durham – which explains the weird accent. A British player. Well, stone me.

Despite their rarity, British players are often overlooked by the media. For instance, the first biography to be produced on an ice hockey player playing in Britain for many years was on Sheffield import Ken Priestlay, rather than say, his Scottish teammate, Tony Hand, despite the fact that Hand is of equal playing stature, and has contributed far more to the British game. Perhaps because they are so familiar to us, British players don't seem to provoke the same level of interest. In Ian Cooper's case, there is the added factor that with an equally successful brother also playing, defenceman Stephen, he has tended to be viewed as part of a duo rather than an individual. This has, perhaps, overshadowed his personal achievements. After Hand, Ian Cooper is the only other player trained in Britain to have amassed over 1,000 league points. In his career so far, he's won dozens of trophies and played for the national team more times than any other player in the modern game. He's probably the best English forward of all time. In a league packed full of stars from overseas, his story is as remakable as anyone's. In fact, when you come to look at it, it is even more so.

To the point of cliché, every kid in it without each other, I wondered. 'If we'd given the same commitment, had there just been one of us, then I think we'd have made it. But I don't know if we'd have tossed it aside halfway through had there been no company. I don't think I draggggk I dragmuch the same story, only instead of hockey, it is football that every boy is supposed to live for. In Durham though, unusually for a town that size, they didn't have a professional football team. What they did have though, were the Durham Wasps, a side which was to dominate British hockey for many years. One bank holiday in the mid '70s, the Cooper family went along to watch a game and their two boys, Stephen, who was eight or nine at the time, and his brother Ian, who was a couple of years younger, were massively impressed.

'We already skated, and we decided we wanted to have a go,' recalls Ian. 'So we got ourselves a pair of second-hand skates, and an old stick. In Durham, you could have a blast after the game, so we started like that.' At around the same time, the Crowtree Leisure Centre, in Sunderland, opened its doors, and the boys divided their time between the two rinks. Athough there was plenty of ice time available, there was little in the way of a structured system for kids to learn the game. 'There was a bit of a void in the junior system then,' says Cooper, understating things a tad. 'The [junior] team in Durham, I think, was under 20s at the time. And that was it, to cover any age from five years old to 20 years old.' Help, however, was close at hand. In hockey folklore, stories abound of kids making it to the NHL because their parents built them backyard rinks to play in. The Coopers' parents took it a step further, and helped build an entire *league* for their kids to play in.

'My parents took on the junior club. Fundraising, fixtures, travel, and other arrangements. More and more clubs were starting up these junior teams, and so a league was started.' Without their support, Cooper feels, he wouldn't have made it. 'Yeah, that was what got us there. From the age of seven up to the age of sixteen, we travelled 14 miles to the rink every day, except Mondays.' Of course, this kind of dedication and support for a child's sporting ambition is hardly confined to hockey. In other sports too, parents are known to make enormous sacrifices in order to help their offspring realise their dreams. In football, especially, it can be a very lucrative move. Almost as soon as a young kid shows a real talent for the game, little £ signs can start to roll in their parents' eyes. But this was a bit different. There was no scheming for future riches here. The Coopers couldn't plan ahead for a career in hockey for their boys, after all, no one else at the time was getting a career from playing hockey. 'There were three imports a team who scraped a living off it, and nobody else got paid back then, so we never thought it would be professional – especially to this level. I think it was just we were dead keen. They enjoyed watching it, seeing us progress, and they were happy to be involved.' Were they doing it then for the love of the game? 'Love of the kids,' was his simple response.

From the moment the kids started playing, hockey came to dominate the Coopers' lives. Presumably, it was just a case of school then hockey for them both? 'It was just hockey *then* school, I think. Nothing else. Absolutely nothing else,' he recalls. So what was it that appealed so much? 'I've no idea what consumed me back then. It was just enthusiasm, I suppose. Just being a kid. But looking at the game now, and seeing other sports, and having played other sports, I think hockey combines pieces of every sport and that's what makes it complete. It's aggressive, it's fast, it's very skilful. Quite often it's like a game of chess and you've got to use your mind. It's everything. Everything that a sportsperson can be, is required in hockey. I think that's what attracts you to it at a young age, although at that age you don't know what it is, I suppose.' There was also the fact that all that equipment and gear must have looked pretty cool to impressionable eyes. 'Yeah, I guess it was quite . . . glamorous. I don't know. I don't know if it was in my nature to play something that was contact. I hadn't really done a lot of that at school. Football, cricket, whatever, you don't really get the chance to hit each other, and I think I found that attractive, because I don't really mind that aspect of it.'

In many respects, the Coopers' early hockey experiences mirrored those of many players who have gone on to make a living at the game. The dedication, the countless hours of practice, the sacrifices made by the whole family. But you have to remember that this wasn't Canada, where thousands of kids were going through the same thing. This was England. Here, kids grew up wanting to be Bobby Charlton, not Bobby Hull. For the Coopers the wider hockey world was something beyond their reach. Their heroes weren't so much drawn from the NHL, but from the Ice Stadium in Durham. 'We started hearing about the NHL and stuff, obviously taking an interest, and watching it on TV whenever it was on, but apart from that it was just teams the Wasps played against. The Scottish teams, Nottingham, Streatham.' And so in this respect, compared to the rest of the players in today's Superleague, the Coopers' upbringing was unusual. Whilst most of them have flown in over the Pond, in hockey terms, at least, the Coopers were to emerge from a small one. And they weren't the only ones.

Just as the Cooper brothers made their way up through the ranks, another local family, the Johnsons – with sons Anthony and Stephen, and later Shaun – were also making a big impression. 'Durham had a lot of good juniors, and we came through the junior system with the Johnson brothers,' Cooper remembers. 'And at that time our junior teams were excelling on the back of theich was to dominate British hockey for many years. One bank holiday in the mid '70s, the Cooper family went along to watch a a game and their two boys, Stephen, who was ei or 9 at the time, and his brother Ian, who was a couple of years younger, were mang players springing up around them, it was only a matter of time before the Wasps decided to use them. Stephen, the oldest, was first to get his chance, making his debut for the Wasps in the 1982/83 season. It was to prove a spur to the others. 'He was playing for the Wasps when he was 13,' Ian remembers. 'Obviously, his getting into the Wasps at a young age probably gave me a little bit of encouragement to work hard, keep going – though at that stage I'd already been playing for years and years. There was no way I was going to give it up or anything.' Looking back on his own career, Ian certainly feels that having a brother who also played helped him. Sure, there was a degree of rivalry between them, but plenty of support too. Would they still have made it without each other, I wondered. 'If we'd given the same commitment, had there just been one of us, then I think we'd have made it. But I don't know if we'd have tossed it aside halfway through had there been no company. I don't think I dragged him along, or he dragged me along, we both loved it so much I think we'd have done it on our own if the other one had not been there. Although it certainly helps.' Surely though, I thought, there must have been times when one of them must have felt like giving up and so needed the support of the other. 'No, I don't think there was. I don't think I ever, ever thought that. I played other sports at school, but I was a hockey player and that was it.'

Two seasons after Stephen had made the Wasps' first team, Ian Cooper started to creep into the team as well. It was a gradual process. 'For a long time I sat on the bench – and never moved.' That's not to say he wasn't getting any ice time somewhere else. 'At the time, whenever the juniors played, I played for them. Whenever the Hornets, which was the Wasps' reserve side, played, I played for them, and I was also sort of sitting on the bench for the Wasps. And training for all three.' Ian's first season, the 1984/85 campaign, finally saw the Wasps realise their earlier promise and become the best side in Britain as they clinched the Heineken Premier League title. It was to be the first of nine major trophies they were to win in the next four seasons as they became a dynasty. Although competition for places was fierce, Cooper found that he was increasingly being given a shift here and there to show what he could do.

'We started going out and trying to prove ourselves. During games, if one player, or one line, was doing badly or not trying hard enough, we'd be given a chance. And when you're given that chance you've got to take it, and try to hold on to that spot if you can. That's what we did. We ended up forming a line together, me and the two Johnson brothers, Stephen and Anthony, and that was what was called the "Kid Line".' This line, sometimes also with Stephen on defence, would at first just be used towards the end of games, in order to give a bit of experience, but as they all developed they were increasingly used at more significant stages, and pretty soon, whilst still only

16 or 18 years old, they were coming up against lines made up entirely of imports. More than that, they were holding their own.

'We had to just go out there and work as hard as we possibly could. Quite often we'd end up scoring goals against other import lines, and that would frustrate other teams. They'd see these three kids coming on, and doing well, and that would motivate the rest of our team, and our crowd, and give us a boost.' Of course, for a coach, using a line of youngsters made sense. As well as helping develop their skills by putting them in against supposedly superior lines, it could also act as punishment for established players who perhaps had got complacent. 'I think it's a bit of everything,' agrees Cooper. 'It gives the senior players who've been benched an opportunity to come back and show they can do it, and it gives us a chance to develop, and show that we're ready. The coach can use it whatever way he likes, or take from it whatever he likes.'

In his first season, where he saw the ice only fleetingly, Cooper had managed to grab five points in 19 games. In the next two seasons, with the 'Kid Line' increasingly used, he was to rack up over 100. By his fourth season he had graduated to playing on the first line alongside imports like Rick Brebant. They were the kind of players Cooper could learn plenty from. 'Back then it was three imports on the team and everyone aspired to that level. Everyone tried to raise their game, and the speed, and fitness. You had a benchmark to aim for. The imports generally coached juniors back then, helped practices. So we did learn from them.' Not that that teaching need be explicit – it wasn't as though he was being shown specific moves or tactics, but more a sense of the dedication required. 'Just the constant training and playing alongside those players. Attitude, and professionalism, what it takes to move to that next level.'

Of course, there were always detractors. Some fans resented imports. Not only did they get paid to play, whilst Brits were lucky to get expenses, but they hogged the puck, the ice and the limelight. A few of the players were less than enamoured too, as

Cooper concedes – though they were always very much in the minority. 'Oh, I'm sure there were one or two, who felt they were pushed out. But there were two or three lines of players on each team, and only three Canadians, so I think if you were capable, I don't think it was that difficult to break into a team.' Indeed, looking back on those days, the British player had every opportunity to establish himself. There wasn't any money in it, which meant that players were part-time, but at least there was plenty of ice time. However, change was around the corner.

In 1986, the Cardiff Devils were formed, and their ambitious player-manager John Lawless thought, not unreasonably, that the best route to success was to sign the best players. Okay, so I'll admit that that probably doesn't sound like the most radical strategy you've ever heard, not exactly the kind of thing that would have had Anatoli Tarasov scratching his head in awe, but at the time, in what seems a rather naive world now, it was pretty devastating stuff. Of course, everyone stole imports from each other all the time. Everyone knew they were just mercenaries and obviously expected nothing else from them, but Brits? Well, what was the point? It was imports that scored all the goals, and anyway, the Brits were local lads with jobs and families. You couldn't expect them to move. Why would they want to leave for another team anyway? Sure Ian Cooper had done well at Durham, winning titles and scoring goals and that, but he had a job there with an international electrical wholesale company. Why would he ever want to give that up? Imagine the shock then, when in 1988, both Stephen and Ian Cooper left the double-winning Durham Wasps to join First Division no-hopers the Cardiff Devils. Shock? In Durham there was palpable outrage . . .

'We'd done well in Durham,' Cooper modestly recalls. 'We'd just won trophies, and had both played regularly and got a little bit of money for doing it, we both had jobs, and John Lawless made us an offer and we didn't really think that much of it, at first. The fact that we'd have to leave home, and pack in good jobs, we thought it would be silly to do. So we said, "Well, if the Wasps can give us a little bit extra, we'll just stay . . ." You know, we'd be at home. We thought it would be the best place for us. So we went in and asked for a bit more – not the level of wages that Cardiff were offering, just to improve on our expenses really, and, uh, we were laughed at. So we took up John's offer, and that was the end of it . . . ' Except that it wasn't the end of anything, really. It was the beginning.

At around the same time, in Canada, the hockey world was stunned when the news of 'The Trade' broke out. However, this wasn't the story involving the Coopers, but the slightly bigger story of the Edmonton Oilers' owner Peter Pocklington trading Wayne Gretzky to the Los Angeles Kings for $15 million plus several players. In North America, the story was big, big news. TV programmes were interrupted mid-air to bring live pictures of the press conference. In America, because of Gretzky's presence, hockey was to boom where it had never boomed before. In Canada, a nation mourned as its most famous resident was lost to the American dollar. (In *The Edmonton Sun* that day, it wasn't just front page news. A banner at the bottom of the front page told readers that the story was continued on 'Pages: 2, 3, 4, 5, 6, 10, 18, 19, 23, 30, 36, 37, 38, 39, 40, 41, 42, 43, 46 and 47'). Ten years on from that trade, it is clear that it irrevocably changed the game in North America. Sport had become big business. And ice hockey was a sport like any other in that respect. Questions had been raised in the Canadian parliament. But no one could see anything legally wrong with the trade. Just because it *felt* wrong that a certain player should go somewhere else because of money, didn't mean that it *was* wrong. Even if it just wasn't right . . .

In British hockey, the Cooper signings had a similar effect in some quarters. So, okay, British hockey was tiny in scale compared to the game in North America, but in relative terms its impact was the same. There was more money coming into the game now, like it or not, and things were changing. As the standard of British players improved, and their impact on just who won what became more profound, it seemed only natural that if some of them were becoming as good as imports, then they should be paid as well as imports. The Coopers hadn't been the first Brits to move to another team, but they were certainly the most prominent, and the move set certain people's minds ticking. 'I'm sure if it didn't affect the players, it affected the coaches,' remembers Cooper. 'Because the coaches started thinking about it. They started thinking, "Well, one or two British players would boost our team. We've got as good imports as anyone else, but if we got a couple of good British players it would really strengthen the team." So I think it opened up a few opportunities for British players.'

At the time, however, the ramifications of the move were hard to grasp. I asked Cooper if he had realised what an effect the move would have on the game. 'I don't think so. I didn't really realise what impact it would have on hockey and the rest of the league. We just took it as a chance to play more hockey, and get paid for doing it. It enabled us to stop work and concentrate hard on hockey.' However, the ensuing uproar was hard on them, and was something that neither had expected. 'We were very surprised,' he admits. 'We weren't trying to hold Durham over a barrel or anything.' (As if two guys called Cooper would ever do that.) 'We saw that perhaps that was the way it was going to go, that there was more and more money coming into it, and Durham were just, I dunno, not prepared to pay, so we took our chance with Cardiff.'

Overnight, Cardiff had suddenly taken over from the Wasps as the most loathed team in the league. Durham had been resented because they had enjoyed so much success. Cardiff started to get it because everyone else thought they were trying to buy it. 'We got a lot of stick around the league – Cardiff as a club, and John did, the chequebook thing. But all he was doing was paying the players what he thought they were worth, and putting on entertainment for the sell-out crowds in Cardiff. That's all he was doing.' Not everyone saw it that way, of course. When the Coopers went back to play in Durham with the Wasps, their reception was chilly, to say the least.

'We got lots of stick when we went back to Durham each time,' Ian recalls, ruefully. As a local lad, it must have been particularly hurtful to him, I suggested. 'Yeah, it was – but it was motivating as well, at the same time. Obviously people had heard stories, and different sides of it. But once you got one of those people down and told them the way it happened, I think people understood. But there were still a lot of people who were very hateful towards us.' The stick they got was fairly easy to understand, even if it seems harsh now. The Wasps had been the dominant side of the time, and people had been stung by what they saw as a betrayal by two local players they had nurtured since an early age. The fact that these boys had been good enough to play the game professionally, but that the club had refused to recognise that, never came into it. Cooper understood their feelings, even if some of it did overstep the mark. 'Some of the fans were just doing it because, you know, that's what fans do. They jeer the opposition, whatever. Some wished us well on our way, but there was a good portion of them that really sort of started the hate campaign against us.' So what was their reaction when, two years later, the Coopers were to move back to Durham? 'Oh, they welcomed us with open arms . . .'

Before that day though, the Coopers had work to do in Wales. Trying to put the furore behind them, they concentrated on the playing side. For Ian, even though he had dropped down a division, he felt he had plenty to prove. 'I think at the time, John was more interested in Stephen, because he had proved himself longer at the highest level. I was a little bit of an unknown quantity, and John sort of, I think at the time, threw me into the package to attract Stephen. He used me as a bit of leverage. Give them both jobs and see how it goes.' Fortunately, for Ian, it went pretty well. 'I got more ice time to prove myself. I'd been used to playing to a higher standard, so I was more than capable of playing in the First Division. We gained promotion which gave us a lot more credibility, and next year the Premier Division title, which was even better.'

If it all seems like it had gone smoothly at this point, it should be remembered that there had been a lot of pressure on the Coopers, and the rest of the Devils, to perform. They had been the chequebook club after all, and a lot of reputations were at stake. Not least those of the Coopers. Failure here would have meant going back to the day job. Promotion from the First Division had obviously been important, but it was the second season, when the Devils upset the league and won the Premier Division title at their first attempt that really justified Lawless's faith in his players. Even before this momentous achievement had really sunk in, a few more gobs were smacked when the Devils won a dramatic shoot-out at Wembley against the Murrayfield Racers to clinch an improbable double at their first attempt. 'No one thought we were going to be really capable of playing in the Premier Division,' remembers Cooper. 'Teams had done it before, they'd won the First Division, come up, then got sent straight back down, or finished dead last. But even the bookmakers had us at 100–1 to win the league and the play-offs, and I think everyone else sort of took our chances the same. Apart from us.' This faith was to be amply rewarded after many of the Devils had put their money where their mouths were, and took advantage of the bookmakers' rashness. 'I won £660, off the double,' Cooper cheerfully says. 'I got them both at 33–1, so I was a bit later than everyone else. Stevie Moria had it at 100–1, as did a few supporters. A couple of supporters made tens of thousands.'

So given how outlandish this success had been, what did Cooper think was the reason for it? 'I think it was just the fact that John brought such a good group of guys together. He brought in Steve Moria, Shannon (Hope), second year he brought Doug McEwan in, but he had British guys sort of in from all over the country. He had guys from Aviemore, he had us from Durham, players from Bristol, and everyone was in this strange Welsh city they didn't know much about, and we sort of all stuck together as a team. We ate, slept and drank together as a team, and bonded really well from the start. And after that first year in the First Division there was no stopping us.' While this made sense, it did fly in the face of those who always argued that you got greater commitment from local players.

'I think we were fortunate to get the right group of players, the right personalities. We had a good team spirit in Durham, but everyone was *from* Durham. They sort of came to the rink, then went home and had their own lives away from the rink. Whereas in Cardiff, we didn't know anyone apart from each other so we sort of spent a lot more time together and got on better as a team.' However, this second season, where the Coopers had pretty much silenced their critics – especially in Durham – was to be the end of their stint in Cardiff. The Wasps, stung by the Welsh side's success, decided to reassess the merits of paying the Coopers what they had asked for. After two seasons away, the prodigal sons were to return. Although not quite as seismic as their previous move, it still surprised those who thought they had been happy in Cardiff.

'Well, we were,' admits Cooper. 'One of the sponsors in Durham started negotiating on Durham's behalf for us, and he offered us more money than we'd made the year before to go back to Durham, which shocked us – bearing in mind that they wouldn't give us better expenses the year prior to that. He said, "Well, it's not only the money. The attitude of the ownership's changed. We've got a new rink planned. Work's going to start within two years." We were made lots of promises. We thought, "Well, hey. We can play at home again. Make better money. They've got a new rink coming. Why not?" John said, "Well, I can match the money, but I can't do any more. It's up to you guys, really. I'm not going to stand in your way." So we said, "Fine." It was an opportunity to play at home and he wished us luck and let us go on our way, which was pretty good of him. He had helped us with our careers and he was happy for us to progress.'

The effects of their return were almost immediate. After a disappointing year previously, which had seen the departure of the Johnson brothers amid a certain amount of rancour, the Devils secured the Grand Slam, with the Coopers and imports Brebant and Mike Blaisdell leading the way. The next year saw them retain three of their four trophies. Everything on the ice seemed to be going well, but off it old problems were starting to resurface. The Coopers started to get itchy skates once again.

'The promises that were made didn't really materialise – apart from our salary,' Cooper explains. 'There was no new rink. Management attitudes hadn't really changed that much. John Lawless popped up again and we went back to Cardiff.'

Clearly, there was something about Cardiff that suited Ian and his brother. He recalls his first game back in Wales whilst still with the Wasps – a marked contrast to his earlier receptions in Durham. 'The first game I played back in Cardiff, I got a standing ovation. The crowd just seemed to appreciate the years I'd played for them.' This was somewhat anomalous. After being hounded by some of the crowd in his hometown, the crowd in Wales had treated him as if he were one of their own. The fact that he had left them for their rivals did not seem to dent this affection. 'I don't know, maybe it was because I was from Durham that the Cardiff fans expected it to happen at some stage, and were happy that I'd come down from my home all the way to Cardiff and helped out. It was a different situation. People had never done it from Durham before.' Whatever the reason, it certainly wouldn't have made the brothers' subsequent return to Wales any less palatable.

The second move to Cardiff, alleged by the press at the time to be for a salary in the region of £30,000, with a signing on bonus of £10,000–£15,000 might have seemed like another gamble for the Devils. If it was, it paid off. After two Cooperless years without a trophy, the Devils promptly won the Grand Slam. The next season, they won the double. Clearly, the Coopers were talismanic when it came to silverware. At this point in their careers they had won 18 major trophies each in just ten seasons, which, let's face it, is taking the piss. It couldn't go on for ever. In 1995 the Sheffield Steelers worked out how to win things without any Coopers when they won the league and cup double. They followed that season up with their own Grand Slam. The era of the arena had well and truly arrived, and there had been an undeniable shift in the balance of power.

Increasingly, professionalism was taking over the game. As the Superleague drew closer it became clear that the way forward – at the top level, anyway – was going to be with squads of full-time professionals, and as restrictions on the use of imports and reclassified players lessened it also became clear that many British players were going to be squeezed out. Whilst the writing on the wall had been evident for some time, the pace at which this change now came about took many by surprise. 'It did change quite fast,' remembers Cooper. 'Players were obtaining British passports, playing in the national team, teams were signing more imports and more foreign players. At the time, you don't see it happening. You don't realise the consequences.' The consequences were that past glories now counted for nothing. Whilst before, the Coopers had been able to dominate, they now found they had to compete. No longer were they battling for places against other British players, now they were battling against the imports. There were no guarantees any more. Brown trousers time?

'All I could really focus on was that I had established my position at that level, and I wanted to keep a hold of that. And whatever the Canadians were doing, to play at that level, or to get better. Whatever they did, I tried to do as well or better. I just tried to put in the work rate, and the fact that I didn't have to work off ice meant that I was able to put in the commitment to try and keep at the top level.' After years of cruising their way through British hockey, suddenly the Coopers had a real challenge on their hands – though if the new imports flooding the game posed a threat, they also showed the Coopers the way forward. As better and better players arrived, so Ian was able to raise the level of his own game. In the past, the standards of many of the imports had been questionable, but there was no denying that the latest wave was taking the game to a much higher standard than had been seen in Britain before – and as the level rose, those players who were able to keep their heads above water found that they were playing better than ever. 'In the past you got imports who just got the jobs because of their resumés. There were, and are, better British players out there. But those type of guys generally didn't last too long. I think the quality was always improving. The guys who were coming in generally had better attitudes towards the game. That rubbed off on you as well.'

Of course, not every player was able to keep pace with the new game. Many would still have jobs, and would be understandably reluctant to let them go in the face of an uncertain and fast changing game. In Ian Cooper's case, hockey *was* his job. Exciting though the challenge of playing Superleague hockey was, the greater spur was simply that his livelihood was now under threat – a situation which he concedes actually helped him. 'I think you've got to look at it that way every year, regardless of other imports. I think you're always fearful of your next contract. I think we always have been. I've tried not to be complacent.' Anyway, none of this was new to him. To an extent he had already been through the same battle with the national side.

A few years previously, in 1989, the Great Britain side had decided to re-enter international competition after several years in the hockey wilderness, with both Coopers in unsurprising attendance. The annual World Championships are staged in mini leagues, and Britain had to enter the fray on the lowest rung, Pool D. At that time, the team, coached by Terry Matthews, was composed entirely of British players, though under the rules they were allowed to pick some Canadian players, providing they satisfied certain criteria regarding how long they had played in Britain. In this first year, Britain narrowly failed to gain promotion, and in the second year, new coach Alex Dampier took advantage of the ruling to pick five Canadians in his squad of 21 players. Promotion was secured – although as Britain won every game by at least ten goals, I'm not sure they were needed, but the ball was rolling.

After two seasons in Pool C, Britain won promotion to Pool B with a squad that had eight dual-nationals in a squad of 22, but as the opposition got tougher, so did the chances of British players making the squad. The team that took to the ice for those Pool B games had five new caps, all of them dual-nationals, and when, incredibly, that team gained promotion to the giddy heights of Pool A, the number was swiftly upped once again so that of the squad of 23 players, only eight were 'British'. Obviously, competing against the likes of Canada and

Jim Hrivnak at the office, Manchester 1997

Sheffield Steelers dressing room, Cardiff 1994

Battle dress, 1994

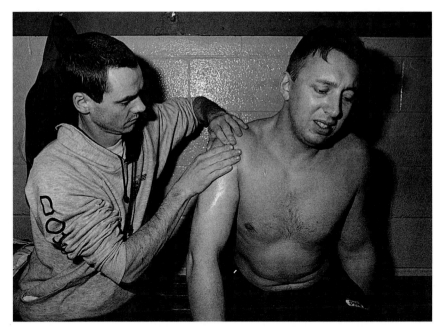

Massage, 1994

Stretching, 1994

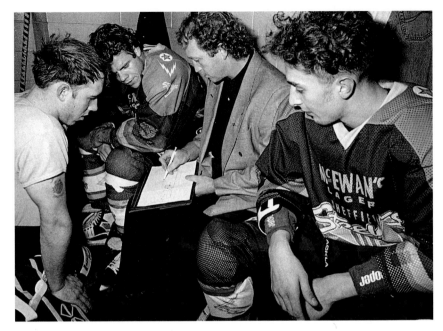

Dampier's game plan, 1994

Steelers' bench, 1994

V for Victory, 1997

Rob Wilson, 1995

Out to battle, Manchester 1997

Tim Cranston, 1994

A big hand from the home
support, Manchester 1997

Ayr's Joey Mittelsteadt, 1997

Goalmouth scramble, Manchester v. Ayr, 1997

Screaming boy, Manchester 1997   Crèche, Manchester 1997

Manchester Arena, 1997

Ivan Matulik, 1997

Goal. Storm v. Ayr, 1997

Russia for the first time in many years, was a pretty daunting task and although both Stephen and Ian managed to register points in the competition, the first 'Brits' to do so at that level since 1962, Britain were promptly relegated to Pool B, where they have so far remained.

The success of the British team in achieving promotion, although heady, had not been without cost. As more dual-nationals had been drafted in, so the resentment amongst some British players had risen. In short, a lot of them felt that the whole idea of a national side with so few Brits lacked credibility, and some, for a variety of reaons, wanted no part in it. Cooper though, had been proud to take part. 'Again, I didn't really sit back and analyse it. I was just thanking God that I'd been able to keep my place. I was just trying to keep working hard to stay ahead of the next import, or the next reclassified player who might take my place on the national team. Obviously, different people had different views on it. It was unacceptable to some players. Some got pushed out. Some players chose not to play for the GB team.'

The most notable absentee from the national side has been Tony Hand who, since 1994, has declined to play for Britain. Whilst sympathetic to his reasons for doing so, Cooper has never felt like following suit. 'I always felt, you know, this is what I'm playing hockey for. Regardless of who else is playing there. I'm going to try and get my place. Then at least I can say I've played at the highest level possible. You represent your country – some things you don't agree with, but at the end of the day if those guys satisfy the national governing body, and the International Ice Hockey Federation, then you've got to at some stage accept that they are British. I still wanted to play for my country.' To an extent, the debate over whether or not to go with an all-British side was a moot point anyway. Legally, if someone has a British passport then they are entitled to be treated the same as anyone else. End of story.

'The guys who played are British,' says Cooper. 'You could have said "You're not playing. You've got a British passport, but you're not playing." I mean now you'd be breaking the law and all kinds. The coach is given the duty of putting together the best team he can – that's what got us to Pool A – we certainly wouldn't have made it to Pool A without the use of reclassified players. There may have been a few dubious choices along the way, who got picked and which British players got left out for which reclassified players, but it's not an argument I can take up.' Besides, as a very wise man once said (Ian Brown from the Stone Roses) 'It's not where you're from that counts. It's where you're *at*.' The guys who played for Britain, Cooper feels, played with just as much heart, passion and pride as anyone else. If they really wanted to play for Britain, and were entitled to do so, and good enough, then it was hard to knock them.

From his own point of view, Cooper's experiences with the Great Britain team were beneficial in more ways than one. Having to fight for his place against imports undoubtedly helped him to do it again domestically when the Superleague era began, but more than that, it also helped improve him as a player. As well as learning from his teammates by their example and application, he had also started to get some decent coaching once he hooked up with the national team. I asked how often he had been coached up to that point. 'I couldn't say I was really coached technically . . . well, I could almost say, never. Not until I played for GB under Peter Woods or Alex Dampier.' Prior to that, despite all the success he had enjoyed in Durham, he had very little direct, one-to-one help. 'The coaching was just as a group, as a team. There wasn't an awful lot of set-plays and tactics back then. The coaching was very limited. We just went out, and did drills and worked hard. That's basically it.' Now though, in Pool A, he had played against the likes of Paul Kariya and Alexi Yashin. Inevitably, he had gained from the experience. 'You just start looking at the game a little differently, you know, when things are pointed out to you by coaches. You start to get a better grasp of the technical side – mainly when you start playing against teams who are superior to yourself.'

Given that Cooper has managed to survive in Superleague hockey, despite never having had the benefit of the kind of early coaching or training that his rivals have enjoyed, the obvious question is whether he and Stephen might have been able to carve out professional careers in North America had they been nurtured the same way, or had they had access to some good coaching at an early age. 'Not from this side of the water,' feels Cooper. 'I'm playing in a league with a bunch of ex-NHLers, or people who have, at some time, aspired to play NHL. So I think if I'd have been on that side of the water I would have aspired to it as well. Whether it would have happened is a different story. We did try and emigrate, when I was about 12, I think. But that didn't come off.' But presumably, the coaching would have made a difference to the kind of player he is today. 'It would have made a big difference,' he admits.

And of course, he's not the only one who must be wondering 'What if . . . ?' In 1986 Tony Hand was drafted by the Edmonton Oilers, but it was a failure to adjust to Canadian lifestyle, rather than a lack of ability that stopped him getting a chance. Given that he has consistently proved himself to be the best player in British hockey over the years, and that he has played amongst many guys who did manage to play in the NHL, the obvious conclusion to draw is that he would have been good enough. So far, he is the only player trained in Britain ever to be drafted, but as Cardiff youngster Stevie Lyle takes a shot at it too, it is hoped he is merely the first. There are those who have said no player from Britain will ever make it in the big league, but Cooper hopes they are proved wrong. 'I think through my career the chance has been very limited. But with the success of the Superleague, and the recognition it's getting throughout the world, if there are players playing here now who are good enough they might get spotted over the coming years as more people are keeping an eye on what is happening over here.'

But it's hard to say whether the chances of that happening have improved or not. Whilst the British players who are playing in the Superleague are playing at a higher level than ever before, and certainly there are more people involved in the game with the kind of coaching experience needed to bring them on, there are fewer of them than ever making it that far.

It's no coincidence that Hand, Lyle and the Coopers had all played for their hometown sides before they were 16, but as Superleague becomes more and more import-based it's nigh on impossible to imagine a British teenager breaking into the league now. Of course, there are few 16-year-old kids anywhere in the world who could play at Superleague level, but in other countries they would still have plenty of leagues for youngsters to play in. The future of the British player is something that Ian Cooper is very mindful of. 'You go out there and you might be the only British player on the ice, playing against a whole team of Canadians. It's in my mind all the time.

'It saddens me to see two teams take to the ice without a British player – a British trained player – among them, when I know there are players in the Premier Division who are capable of playing. Albeit, some of them are not willing to give the commitment to reach that level, though some of them are – they just haven't been given the opportunity. And the opportunity is reducing all the time for those guys.' Indeed, increasingly, it seems the window is getting smaller. 'The chance of juniors coming through the system is reducing even more quickly, because there is a little bit of a void between junior development and ISL. It's all dependent on how the league below is structured, and how successful it is, you know, and what sort of opportunities the coaches on Superleague teams are prepared to give to Premier league players.'

So how important is it, from a fan's perspective, that there are young British players coming through? 'Hopefully, it's what the crowd want to see,' says Cooper. 'You want to see local lads coming through. You want to be able to relate to that player out there. You don't just want a constant stream of new faces flying in. You might as well just watch NHL on TV.' This is a key point. When the public feel they can relate to a sporting personality, that they know something about him, then they take a greater interest. The casual channel-hopper, flicking through his TV options, might just alight on ice hockey one night. Now this guy has an attention span of about two seconds. Something has to grab him. If he sees a player he recognises, or hears a name that is familiar, then he is more likely to hang around and watch a bit. And the more he watches, the more he learns. The more he learns, the more he is likely to care what happens. We are all likely to take more interest in something when we know one of the protagonists – for instance, I once watched an episode of the interminable *Ready, Steady, Cook,* simply because I knew someone who was appearing on it.

It doesn't matter if we like that person or not. After all, as many people tuning in to watch Prince Naseem Hamed want to see him get his stupid, cocky, arrogant face punched in as to see him triumph; but the point is, they are interested in him because they know something about him. To an extent, it's a *catch-22* situation, as sport needs the media to build characters, and the media will want to see characters before it decides to promote the sport, but the more 'characters' there are in a sport, the more people will want to watch it. Dull though snooker is, in the mid '80s it was tremendously popular because, like a soap opera, it was full of characters the public could relate to. Today, the sport is, technically, better than ever, but it is in some decline because the viewing public can't differentiate between one acne-ridden millionaire superstar and another. Of course, to the converted, all of this is less important. The fans of Sheffield or Manchester aren't going to mind if all their players come from Iraq, and have the charisma of Trevor Brooking in a coma, providing they cut the mustard on the ice. It is the wider public, the ones who aren't knowledgeable about the game, the ones the game needs to sell itself to, who need to feel they can relate to a certain player – and if that player is British there is more chance of that happening.

There is also more chance of British youngsters taking up the game if they can see British players at the top level, a point Cooper feels is important also. 'I think so, yeah. It affects junior players starting out, junior players who are aspiring to become top level players. They need to know they can reach that level. That there is a route up that ladder all the way to the top, otherwise they'll take up some other sport, or focus on college, or a job or career. They need to be able to see that clear route to the top. Or at least a chance to take that clear route. At the moment, there isn't that chance. And I think there are a few different people, or groups, to blame for that. Not naming any names, but there's been a few decisions taken down the years that haven't made it easier. There are coaches and clubs who have not been willing to give these guys a chance and then work with them to bring them on to that other level. And there's also, more recently, the governmental department which sort of sat back and allowed it to happen. The Department of Employment, I feel at the moment, or in recent years, sort of let it happen a bit too easily.'

Whilst there is little that can be done about limiting the amount of British or EC passport holders coming into the game, it certainly seems that it has become too easy to obtain a work permit for some players, particularly when there isn't the need. 'There are so many British and European players, Canadians with residency stamps, or right of abode, who can obtain British passports, that it's just escalated so far now that there's no real control over work permit players. Although I think Superleague are going to try and take that in hand over the next couple of years,' says Cooper. Indeed, at the time of writing, the ISL had announced that they intended to reduce the number of players on each team's roster who needed work permits. Whilst the results of this decision are unlikely to be felt immediately, Cooper does feel it is a step in the right direction. 'It is going to have an effect, and hopefully coaches are going to try and target a few British players in the Premier Division and give them a boost, that encouragement to try and excel and progress to the next level. To give them the coaching, rather than just picking out resumés from agents, and signing guys unseen.'

Regardless of where players come from, however, it is more than just 'on ice' matters that are of concern to Cooper. Since its inception, a few seasons before the arrival of the Superleague, Ian Cooper has been prominently involved with the Ice Hockey Players Association (IHPA), an organisation that tries to protect players' interests, irrespective of where they come from. Although there are many fantastic aspects to being a professional ice hockey player, job security has never been one of them. The life of a professional athlete is notoriously difficult to predict, and whilst some players may feel they are safe as houses, closer inspection has tended to reveal that the houses in question are the ones hugging the tottering North Yorkshire coastline. At some point in the future, players are likely to find themselves dumped into the murky waters below. Whilst it could be argued that this comes with the territory, there's no question that in the past less scrupulous clubs have turned this insecurity to their advantage. Players have been withheld monies, sacked without notice or compensation, had promises broken and been vulnerable to completely losing their livelihoods if injured. In the past, players were often exploited and bullied by some clubs. Sooner or later, they had to stand up for themselves.

'I think there's always been a need for something,' believes Cooper. 'In the past, players have had to fight for what they can get themselves. It was just a way to put a voice out there for the players, and fight for the players' rights and try to improve all aspects of the game for the players. Not in wages terms, but in contractual terms, facilities, everything. Before it was a bit of a dictatorship. Players had no real rights or powers, so they just needed someone to give them a shoulder to lean on, who could help them out in different situations. Someone the teams had to answer to, rather than leaving it to players as individuals.' The year before the ISL was formed, after a couple of years' campaigning, the IHPA had been officially recognised by the BIHA, and membership levels amongst the players was very high. Initially though, when the ISL was formed, it seemed as though the Association had been knocked back a couple of steps, as they would have to start all over again, and the sheer number of new players meant a new recruitment drive was called for.

Happily, though, Cooper is able to report that of the 270 or so players involved at the top end of the game, 250 are members, and the relationship with the ISL is improving all the time. 'We are forging better links with Superleague. The year before the ISL was formed we were given official recognition by the BIHA. We started by pushing for recognition with Superleague – though recognition is something we have already anyway. They meet us, and listen to us, and so just by that we get recognition. The next thing we are striving for is a collective bargaining agreement, which will set down in writing agreements between us and them and them and us. What we must do for them, and what they must do for us. I feel the relationship is improving. It was a difficult job for them because they had to clear up a lot of things they inherited. It's a continual process. I think Superleague will be learning for a lot of years to come, but it will be a continual improvement. Things are certainly getting better.'

Although there are many observers who continue to be critical of the way the game is organised, Cooper isn't one of those people pining for 'the good old days'. In the past, the game was pretty much run by enthusiastic amateurs, and only those with selective memories would like to think things were run better then. Like it or not, as with most other sports you could care to mention, the game is now run by businessmen who, of course, continue to make mistakes and, hopefully, learn from them. But Cooper is in no doubt as to which era of the game he prefers. 'I'm happier with the way it's gone. It's created the opportunity for players to do it full-time, and do it for a living. And everything in and around the game is more professional. Better arenas, people are looked after better, you know you are playing as a professional and you're treated as a professional.' That this was unimaginable just a few short years ago shows how far we've come.

To Cooper, it all seems a long way from days spent chasing a puck in Durham. Other players may have flown thousands of miles to play Superleague hockey, but Cooper has probably had to travel further than any of them to play at this level. It was never something he could have envisaged. 'I couldn't have predicted it was going to change this much. I guess, at that time, I thought it would just plod along. We would continue to do what we were doing for the money we were making.' So is his life as a hockey player better now than before? 'The level is better. The level of play is better. It doesn't necessarily mean the level of wages is better. I was making more money back then than I am now, put it that way.'

This might sound surprising to some, as Ian Cooper now is a better player than he ever was before, but one of the ironies of his career is that even though he helped pave the way for British players to make a living from the game, his own value has gone down, even as he improved. Before, he was competing against a handful of other British players, but now he is so good he is competing against a much bigger pool of players from all over the world. Simple supply and demand has meant that he no longer makes what he once did. He is philosophical about this, though, because he is realistic about the way the game is run now, and if he has to compete against players from Canada, Sweden, America or wherever, then it isn't a problem. The only player he does have trouble competing against is from Durham.

In 1997, John Lawless, then coach at the Manchester Storm, once again managed to entice Stephen Cooper to a new club. This time, Ian stayed put, and for the first time in their lives, the two brothers were pitted against each other in competition. Surely, that must have been strange for him at first. 'Still is. It's not right,' he admits, plaintively. Presumably, when he goes into the corners after the puck and he sees number 55 on an opposition shirt he isn't as determined to knock that player senseless as he might be otherwise. 'No, not really. You're never going to hit him as hard as you'd hit anyone else.' Presumably, that goes both ways. It's just as difficult for Stephen to pile into Ian. 'Um, on and off,' Cooper replies, cautiously. 'It's a bit more difficult for him, because if I don't hammer him, okay, so we might not win the puck and get a scoring opportunity, which isn't a great miss – but if he misses me, and I score, it exposes him. It's a little difficult for defencemen to ease up, which I understand. But I don't tell him that . . . I just complain when he hammers me.'

Just like when they were kids.

SECOND PERIOD

The Third Team

I have a friend, Bill, who has the endearing habit of perpetually disagreeing with everyone. (Yes you do, Bill.) He has a tendency, upon meeting people for the first time, to have raging rows with them within a few minutes. Partly, he does this out of habit, because he enjoys winding people up and getting reactions from them, but he also does it because he believes the only way to ever come to a genuine opinion about anything is to first disagree with whatever it is everyone else says about it, and then later decide what you think yourself. Whilst this might sound a little indulgent – and it certainly seems a good way to make sure you get kicked unconscious outside Withington pubs on a Saturday night, there is some method in his madness. Socrates (the Greek philosopher, not the Brazilian footballer) would seek universal truths by the simple expediency of questioning everything set before him. So, Bill's technique has a noble and long standing history, though I'm not sure how often Socrates got his head caved in when he practised it.

So when I decided to write about referees, that apparently loathsome and insidious group of men who continually stop our favourite team from winning, I decided to take a leaf from Bill's book and try to go against the grain of public opinion. To the general public, referees are a repugnant breed. Pedantic little pseudo-Hitlers. They strut around, drawing attention to themselves and hogging the limelight wherever possible, and their grasp of the rules and mores of the game is tenuous at best. Hmm. I'd set myself a right old challenge to disagree with *that*. Okay. The case for the defence begins.

Ice hockey is the most difficult sport I know of to officiate. In cricket, for example, the crucial action is contained within a small area, and the umpire maintains a static position. The play can easily be anticipated, and the rules are strictly laid down and easy to follow. As long as your eyesight holds out, and you retain the ability to wear 14 jumpers at once in stifling heat, you can continue to be a cricket umpire for many, many years. Football, on the other hand, is more difficult, in that it is refereeing on the run – as the official has to follow the play and the rules, to a degree, are open to interpretation. Everyone agrees that it is monstrously hard to officiate. Ice hockey, though, is harder still. For a start, it is just so damn fast. Players hurtle round the ice at 30 m.p.h., the puck nearer 100 m.p.h. In such a confined playing area the referee's view is nearly always obstructed, and its lack of set-plays makes it more difficult to anticipate the action. Possession of the puck, on average, changes about 120 times during the course of a hockey match. This means the referee is forever twisting and turning, braking and accelerating, reacting and anticipating, to keep up with the play. It's a game played on emotion, which the referee must tap into. Players come on and off the ice surface continually, which the officials must keep track of. And then there are the rules.

How many of us have actually sat down and read the rules to ice hockey? I did once, and frankly, it did my head in. Hockey is a game filled with infractions. However, players move around so fast, and collisions are so inevitable, that to call everything would be to reduce the game to a disjointed, stop-start mockery of continuous expulsions and powerplay goals. The players, and the fans, want the game to flow. They want the action to run as smoothly as possible. They want the ref to turn a blind eye as much as possible, so that what they are watching begins to look something like a game. To let the players decide the outcome of a match. *To let the game flow*. On the other hand, hockey is a game where fervent emotions can boil over in an instant. If there's one thing more scary than an enraged, adrenalin-pumped, six feet four inch defenceman bearing down on you, it's one who happens to be carrying a large stick as well. Hockey can be a dangerous game. The referee is there to try and prevent anyone from getting hurt. Effectively, when a referee consults the rule book, it says 'Use your discretion, mate.' It seems an impossible job. What is going on here? Bring on the witness for the defence.

Considered by many within the game to be the best referee in Britain, Simon Kirkham has been officiating at ice hockey matches for over ten years. He learnt to skate when he was three years old, and took up ice hockey when the Nottingham Panthers were revived after a 20-year hiatus in 1980. He was good enough to play for the Panthers' second team without being 'particularly brilliant', and he could skate fast. When he left Nottingham he continued to follow the game, and spent a lot of time watching the Altrincham Aces, but it wasn't until he moved to Coventry and spent time at the rink there that he was invited to become an official, simply because he was a good skater, and, erm, they were a bit desperate. For someone who had never seriously considered the job before, his progress from then on was swift. A combination of being in the right place at the right time, and having an instinctive aptitude for it, meant that he was rapidly promoted up through the ranks.

'I was lucky enough, within six months of starting it, to go into the top league,' he recalls. 'Mainly because I was a bit older – I was, what, 24 or 25 – so I was a little bit older than most people who take it up. So I progressesd very quickly into the top league. (At the time, the Heineken Premier League.) Within two years I was doing the final, so it was pretty quick.' Such a rapid ascent would probably have been too much for some, but Kirkham took to it like a duck to water. 'I didn't mind. It was a case of "sink or swim" and I swam. But I had good teachers. Good mentors. I picked up a lot from guys like Nico (Toeman), Bob Baumer, Micky Curry, and these are the kind of guys, when you talk to them, that you get feedback from, that you learn a lot from.' Even with good tutors, though, not everyone who tries his hand at it will make a good referee. Assuming that a ref knows the rules, is able to skate properly, is reasonably fit and has decent eyesight, then you would expect him to have all he needs to be a good ref – but no. This is not always the case. Refereeing is a mental discipline, first and foremost. A battle with your own mind firstly, and then with others. It demands certain mental qualities. Unkind fans have long argued that these mental qualities are usually just manifestations of childhood insecurities, or sadistic/masochistic leanings – which is a tad uncharitable, but what a ref really needs is toughness. Mental strength.

'I think you've hit the nail on the head,' says Kirkham. 'You have to be mentally strong, and alert. You have to have your wits about you. You need to be able to project something about yourself. Not arrogance, as that is no help, but confidence. To know that what you are going to call is right. You project something that is right. To have a rapport with the players. And be a good skater, that goes without saying. Nico Toeman, for me is a great ref. Everyone knows where they stand. I mean he has good games, and bad games, everyone does, we've all had them. Mick Curry was another (top British referee, tragically killed in a car crash in 1993). He just had a presence on the ice. Mike Rowe has that authority as well.'

The obvious question, though, is why on earth did he want to take it up in the first place? Let's not get sentimental here. Refereeing is a filthy job. So what was the appeal? 'Well, there was no money appeal, 'cos we hardly got paid anything,' laughs Kirkham. 'I don't know. I just loved it. I used to play hockey, and watch it, and I just got a buzz out of it. Something that I can do, that I've always loved to do – I mean I've always loved skating. And it's something I know I'm good at. I enjoyed doing it. And it was nice to put something back into the sport.' And there were some fringe benefits, too. 'I was a linesman for six years, and I went all over Europe – which I wouldn't have done otherwise. It was a unique position where you get paid to do something you really love doing. Even now, I get to go all over Europe to referee and someone pays me to do it. I love it. It's brilliant.' Though in the early days, it wasn't quite as serious as it is now. 'I used to get a laugh out of it. You used to have local lads playing and it meant more to them, though in the old Heineken League there wasn't so much of the pressure that there is now. The pressure now is tremendous. Completely and utterly different to the old Heineken Days.'

Aah, the old Heineken days. Those were the days of ridiculous scorelines, heavy boozing and something that you hardly ever see nowadays – the British player. No wonder people get nostalgic about it. For Kirkham, it was a different age. 'In the days of the Heineken league, you had more British guys playing, and after the game you'd all go and have a beer together. You'd all talk. And now, as professionalism has crept in, there isn't time to do that.' (It will come as a shock to followers of the game in Sheffield and Manchester, but the culture of drinking in the old league makes today's players look like Quakers.) 'I mean, I know all the British guys still playing at the top, and the ones not playing, and our respect for each other is completely different to that between the Canadians and myself. I don't get any hassle off any of the British guys, and if you compare that to what I get off the Canadians . . . It's a different breed of character, a different breed of people.' Which is presumably a tactful way of saying they don't have as much respect for British refs as the old British players would have done, a point Kirkham concedes. 'They don't know the background. They don't know me, they don't know who I am.' And of course, Kirkham doesn't know them.

When players and refs know each other, it becomes easier for both sides. A player will know where he stands with a referee, and equally important, the referee will know where he stands with the player. Swearing, for example. Some referees will not tolerate being sworn at, while others accept it and indeed may be only too happy to give it back a bit, finding that it helps create a rapport. However, you have to know who you are dealing with, as Kirkham explains. 'A player like Tony Hand, I would not swear at Tony Hand. Now, his brother Paul, you could tell Paul to "Fuck off" all day and it wouldn't bother him.

Tony, however, is a completely different character and would never swear at me. He might say, "Simon, what you call that for? I never hit him . . . " But he'd never swear. Another player might be effing and blinding. A player like (Mike) Bishop, you could just say "Aw Bish, fuck off," and he'd take that and go away, and leave you to it. And the respect is there.'

'If the refs don't respect the players, then the players sure as hell aren't going to respect the referees,' says Ron Shudra, putting the players' point of view across. 'To be a decent referee you have to earn the respect of the players. And that's so simple to do – just by being consistent.' For Kirkham, this consistency and mutual respect is important. Once established, it prevents a lot of problems as players and officials will know each others' game, and trouble, as it were, is headed off at the pass. The Superleague, however, has seen so many players arrive that are new to the British game that Kirkham has to start from square one with many of them. Players who don't know the referee they are dealing with naturally try and see what they can get away with, be it abusing the official, or bending the rules of the game. Kirkham though, is always quick to try and let the players know where they stand. 'They get to learn very quickly – or they're too thick to learn at all. Some players you can just give penalty after penalty after penalty, and they still don't learn. You think to yourself, "What am I doing wrong?" But I always give them one bite of the cherry. If they want to keep biting the cherry then I just tell them "No, I've had enough", give them a penalty and send them to the box. You have to let the player know that he can't carry on doing what he's doing. If he's going to keep yapping to you every five minutes, well first time, tell him, "Okay, you've had your yap, go away, keep it quiet." But if it keeps coming then you give the penalty. You have to tell them; you explain why.'

Kirkham values the chances he gets nowadays to talk to players after the game. 'It is always good when you can talk to, relate to, a player and you can give your side of the argument rather than just taking what he says to you. And you're actually having a good communication there, rather than on the ice, with him having a crack at you, and you having a crack back. Or him having a crack, and you giving him a penalty. It's nice to talk to them. To see them as individuals. I had a good chat with Ken Priestlay about this. He said to me, "Look, Simon, my coach can tell me 20 times not to yap, not to talk to you, but there's certain situations in a game that happen, and I'll just have to have a yap. But you can just turn around and say to me, 'Go away. I'm not interested' – which I do." But you have to realise in a game that they are going to do that. Scott Young, when he was at Kingston, was always yapping, he was unbelievable. I did four games with him, and had to kick him out three times. But he's changed. As long as they're not abusive towards you then I don't really mind. You've got to let the players know where they stand, and sometimes that can be very hard.'

Tough as it might be for referees to put up with abuse from players, at least they have the power to do something about it, be it dishing out a penalty or having a word with the player concerned. It is a different matter when the abuse raining down on an official is coming from the crowd. As it happened, this was a point that was very much on Kirkham's mind too. The night before our interview he had officiated at a Superleague game in Bracknell where the visitors, Sheffield, had won the game in sudden death overtime. The Bracknell fans, obviously irked by this turn of events, vented their frustrations on Kirkham, as though he was the man who had actually scored the game winner himself. 'You get abuse anywhere, at any rink,' Kirkham says, wearily. 'Though at Sheffield you don't hear it 'cos it's so big – unless they're *all* booing you, and at Manchester you don't hear it because you're cocooned in this wall of plexi-glass.'

It is the smaller rinks, though, where the fans are much closer to the action, that the abuse can really rain down. 'You just get on with it. At Basingstoke and Bracknell you get abuse whoever you are. At Bracknell last night, I got loads of abuse from the crowd all night. I was called everything from a horse to a dog. But they've paid their money, and they're entitled to do that. I don't mind that. Except when they start swearing and there's kids involved, then I don't like that. But they can do that. I'm thick-skinned enough. It doesn't bother me. I won't let it bother me. That's what I get paid to do. But you do sometimes wonder, "Why? What have I done to deserve this?" But it goes with the territory. You bounce back.'

Surely though, I suggested, sometimes it must get you down. There must be times, however fleeting, when you think about quitting. Kirkham was candid in his response.

'Yes, I'll tell you. I seriously considered quitting last night. Because I was peeved by this idea that it's always the ref's fault. Never the players'. Not the guy who should have put the puck in the back of the net but didn't. It's the ref's fault.' Aah, well. Now that is a familiar line. The old 'The ref cost us the game' routine. In a sport as emotional as ice hockey, where fans and players are always quick to jump on a scapegoat, and in a country where conspiracy theorist and *X-Files* fans abound, the shadowy, sinister figure of the referee tends to fit the bill nicely.

In a press conference during the 1997 Championship Finals in Manchester, for example (and there are plenty of other teams who have been equally guilty of this), certain Cardiff players expounded at great length on how poor the refereeing was in their semi-final game with Sheffield which – and I'm sure it's entirely coincidental – they lost. At first, it seemed fair enough. No doubt the odd call the other way would have made a significant difference, and you could sense their frustration. But then it went on. For a solid five minutes they crucified the referee in front of the assembled journalists and reporters. Increasingly, it started to look less like criticism and more like petulance. Finally, one of the journalists made the point that Sheffield had played well, and deserved their victory. Oh yeah, the Devils players agreed. They did. They accepted that Sheffield had been the better side. They were careful to go on record that they wanted to take nothing away from the Steelers. But there was no retraction of any of the criticism of the referee, even though it now transpired that they felt they deserved to lose the game anyway. So what, exactly, was the point of slagging off the referee? After such a disappointment, it's understandable that players should be upset, but when the uncomfortable truth may be that their *own* performance was what was lacking, it was a shame that they should heap the blame on the officials. But then, the referee is always such an easy target. No one cares if he gets slagged off.

It is hardly surprising, therefore, that fans are often quick to blame the referees when they hear their own players badmouthing them. Surely if the players think the ref made a mistake then he must have, right? Surely, they know the game better than anyone. 'It's not always my fault,' points out Kirkham. 'I had players from Bracknell come up to me last night and say, "Why didn't you call that?", but then their teammate has admitted that there wasn't anything there. Even teammates see it differently. It's strange when some guys say, "Such and such should be banned," but another guy will go, "Look Simon, there was nothing there." And you think to yourself, "Eh? I know there was nothing there – now, could you please go and tell your teammates what you just told me."' And this is one of the difficulties for a referee. Hockey infractions can be like that optical illusion, the picture of the old hag who, when looked at another way, turns out to be a beautiful woman. 'People can see the same thing, but perceive it differently,' says Kirkham, summing it up quite neatly.

In the main, coaches are less likely to heap the blame on the referee than players. Perhaps, because it is their job to scrutinise their own players' performances honestly, they tend to see things a little more dispassionately. 'It would be very easy to beat up on the referee every night,' admits Kurt Kleinendorst, speaking figuratively, presumably. 'But my track record on questioning their calls is very poor. They are nearly always right. They know the rules better than anyone.' Certainly better than the players themselves, and although few fans would admit it, they know a lot more about hockey than the spectators too. As an illustration, I have a friend who, after watching a frustrating game which our side had lost, complained to me about one of the linesmen. 'That Hanson, he doesn't know anything about hockey.' I pointed out to him that 'That Hanson' was Moray Hanson, the former Murrayfield Racers and Great Britain netminder and, at one point, one of the most famous players in the game. He admitted that he had never heard of him. Ironic, for someone who had just accused an official of not knowing anything about hockey. Whilst it might be an unfair, sweeping generalisation, and undoubtedly one that has been coloured by watching so many games in Manchester where the fans are still learning about the game, it does seem to me that fans know Jack Shit about hockey sometimes.

Another thing that few fans appreciate is how much the referees have in common with the players. Just like players, they have good games and bad games. Sometimes a player will get the feeling, often hours before the game is due to start, that he is destined to have a good game. Refs are exactly the same, though Kirkham admits it's difficult to explain why. 'You just feel right, sometimes,' he says, aware of how odd this must sound to people. 'Everything is right, it feels good.' The flip side of course, being that you get slumps too. 'Games have their own rhythm, they have peaks and troughs, but sometimes you can be out of sync with the game, and you can't go with the flow. Maybe reading too much into plays, or too little, and that's frustrating. I have high standards for myself, and sometimes after a game, if I think I haven't done as well as I should have, I kick myself. Not only for letting everyone else down, but letting myself down too.' This flies in the face of popular opinion, somewhat. The thought that a referee might be admonishing himself after a bad performance doesn't fit too snugly with the image most fans have of the referee manically laughing with evil, despotic laughter and rubbing his hands with glee at the thought of having ruined everybody's evening. It has never crossed most fans' minds that the referee might be just as down as the players after a game has gone badly.

When he has a bad game, Kirkham is wary of bottling things up. 'The way I get out of it is by talking to people, supervisors, colleagues, friends etc. Sometimes you just have to go back to the beginning and reassess yourself. You have to forget everything around you and get into the flow of the game. Immerse yourself. Get involved – well, not involved, because that's the last thing as a ref that you want to do – but so that you are on the outside, making sure the game's played fairly. And played to the rules. But the satisfaction I get is when the players come up to me and say, "Great game, Simon. Well refereed." When I finish a game and know that I've done a good game.'

This idea of the flow of an ice hockey match is one of the key areas to understanding it. Hockey is often a game of momentum, with one side perhaps dominating another for a spell, only for the balance to tip and for the game to slide the other way. Most obviously you can see this in scoring sprees, when suddenly a team can pull away and score two or three goals in a matter of a few minutes, but, more subtly, it applies to the refereeing also. 'It does swing in a game. If you've noticed; in a game, you can call two or three penalties against a side, then it swings the other way, and you call against the other side. And that's sometimes what the players don't understand.' A good referee, or rather, a referee who is having a good game – Kirkham admits even the best refs can struggle sometimes – will be one who understands the flow of a game, and to an extent, is able to understand not only how the game has gone, but to also anticipate where it is going. Although experience obviously helps, it is largely an instinctive thing.

Anyone who has spoken to players about referees will have heard them talk about tempo: 'The ref sets a good tempo.' It is a compliment, of course, suggesting that the ref is in tune with the game, but I feel it also misses a crucial point. The suggestion is that it is the ref who decides what kind of game it is going to be. This is palpably untrue. A referee doesn't dictate the play – he reacts to it. Or at least he should do. Yet the players still seem to feel that it is the ref who sets the tempo. 'Well, they always think it is set by the officials,' agrees Kirkham, 'but I tend to let *them* set the tempo. You can't make your mind up before a game. You can't go in and think to yourself, "I'm going to call this game the same as I did the last one". You have to judge each game on its own merits.

'Sometimes you can go to a game, and straight from the face-off there's a fight. Then it's up to you to say "Right, you're in the box. Any more fights boys, then sorry, you'll be kicked out." The players have set the tempo of the game.' However, even with the tempo set, it will still be up to the ref to decide how he is going to call it, what he will, and will not tolerate. 'They set the tempo, and we call the game according to that tempo.

'We have what we call the line – an imaginary line – that we set. You might say to yourself, right, I'm not going to call any penalties unless this, this and this happens. Or you could set it low, and say, right anything, and I'm going to call the penalty. Or the grabbing and holding, say, maybe call a couple of them just to let them know I'm watching them do it.' It is a balancing act, argues Kirkham. If you call everything then the game will be frustrating and boring to watch, but if you don't call enough it can get dangerous. It is difficult to get exactly right too, because the slightest variation in where that line is set can have a profound effect on how the game is called.

'We set the level of how far they can go. But players are always trying to see if they can get that level to go any higher. They are always trying it on with you,' explains Kirkham. Players realise that a game will have its own standards, and so penalties are not called according to the rules so much, but according to the level set by the game. 'Nine out of ten times, a team will know where that level is. They know that any more than that and you'll call a penalty.' As the tone of a game changes, so can the level of what is and what isn't tolerated. On every shift, players may try to push the envelope back further. To increase the intensity. To see how far they can go, and what they can get away with, without overstepping the level. 'Sometimes, perhaps, we can set the level too high, and by the end of the game it gets too physical,' admits Kirkham. 'We've maybe allowed the level to rise rather than keeping it constant through the game. That is something we are mindful of. You can see if it's gone too far.' Then you can start to see sticks flying.

Players get frustrated by what they see as infractions by the opposition going unpunished. This, in turn, can lead to the players becoming more aggressive in their play. 'That's what a lot of it is,' believes the Steelers' Ron Shudra. 'A lot of it is frustration. You can see it on the players' faces because calls aren't made.' A player can be hacked and slashed several times, but nothing is called because it is within the level. Players don't always see things that way. Eventually, they will start to slash back, and then it can get out of hand. Then the ref has to act quickly to bring the temperature down. 'You can call two or three penalties and bring the level of a game back down again to what it should be,' says Kirkham. Although having said that, it's not the easiest thing for a referee to do, 'Sometimes, in the heat of a game, you can forget where that level was. It's not very often that happens, but I'd be the first to admit that, perhaps on occasion, I've allowed the level of a game to get too far. But, then again, I'm only human. Sometimes you can see something, but before you can call it, something else happens, maybe two or three other penalties happen at once, and by the time you've sorted that out, you've missed the original penalty you were going to call. And I've got to be honest and say, "Look, I made a mistake." And coaches and players will understand that.'

Something that players and fans don't always understand, though, is what they see as inconsistency. 'The [referees] are not consistent,' Ron Shudra feels, echoing a sentiment held by many fans and players. 'One game they'll call everything, the next they'll call nothing. They're not there to make a spectacle of themselves. They're not out there to be the centre of attention. They're there to let the game flow.' Yet this is easier to say than do. The referee cannot call everything he sees without ruining the game (again, the mantra: *Let the game flow*), yet if he calls nothing the game becomes a farce. So some infractions get called, others don't. This can appear random to players – though it usually isn't, and as a result penalised players will often get upset, not because they are innocent (they rarely are) but because they have seen others getting away with it. When a player throws his arms out in disgust at being called, the frustration usually stems from his feeling of 'Why me?' This apparent randomness appears as inconsistency, and is the bane of the players' lives.

Everything, though, has to be taken in context. Referees don't judge calls by the rule book so much as by the circumstances in which they take place. 'I think in any sport it's the same,' says Kirkham. 'I mean, you do call it according to the rule book. It's written there in black and white, but you do have latitude within that to manoeuvre.' The referee doesn't want to be seen as the deciding influence in a game. No one ever paid to watch the ref. It is a players' game. Let them decide the outcome. Hockey is a game of momentum, and a powerplay at a crucial time can alter the course of a game, and often its result; so referees are always going to be mindful of how their reactions can affect a game. In overtime, for instance, when a single error can cost a team the game, referees are loath to call anything because any powerplay goal will invariably be blamed on them. For their part, the players would prefer to settle it five-on-five, and so they expect the ref to put his whistle in his pocket during overtime and only make a call if someone gets their head knocked clean off their shoulders. This context is understood by both players and officials, though there is nothing in the rules about it. But if a referee was to call the game in overtime the same way he would at the start of a match (to be consistent, in other words) then the players would be in uproar. 'How can he do that! He's got to let the game flow!' But there are other contexts which are not so clear cut.

If, for example, it is early in a game, and the referee spots a hook, say, that prevents a breakaway, then he may call it. However, if he saw the exact same incident in a game when one team is so far ahead of the other that a powerplay goal isn't going to make any difference for them, then he is more likely to let it go. Kirkham gives an example. 'It was Cardiff against Basingstoke. It was a nothing game (end of season contest) and Kip Noble was bringing the puck out and got hooked twice. Two different instances of getting hooked. He goes down. But Cardiff don't lose the puck. And he wings at me. I go, "Kip, you're winning 7–2 mate, I'm not going to give that penalty

90

because it's a shit call. Any other game I would have given the penalty." He went, "Okay. Thanks, Simon, for telling me." And then he got on with the game. But in most games, if that had happened, you would have given the penalty. There are so many variants. It's all about possession of the puck, and the severity of how they try to get the puck off them. Okay, a hook here, a hook there, it's not going to hurt anyone. But if it's a slash, or a trip, then that's got to be called. Some of them are black and white. Like high sticks. High sticks and accidental injury – two plus two with an injury, five plus game, or even match.'

On the other hand, if a referee spots an infraction by a short-handed team, he is going to be more reluctant to call it because another penalty would mean a five-on-three, and the chances of a goal, and therefore the referee having had an indirect bearing on the outcome of the game, are increased. Likewise, one infraction may be identical to another that preceded it, but on this occasion, a clear-cut scoring chance was denied, or created. It was more important, even if it was no more severe, and so it gets called even if the first one didn't. You could argue that it was inconsistent, but the truth is that the referee is forced to apply the rules in the context of a game – to apply common sense, in other words, and as a game is always changing, so are the conditions under which different calls are made. How can he be consistent?

Say a player hooks another. The ref doesn't call it. The same guy does it again. Still no call. Then there is another hook, perhaps in retaliation, but the ref calls that one. There are howls of protest from fans and players alike. 'The refereeing is inconsistent,' everyone moans. But if you place those same instances in the context of the game, and where the level of that game might have been set by the referee, then it begins to make more sense. Run through it again. The first hook happens. The referee sees it, but perhaps feels that no advantage was gained or denied, and that it wasn't malicious or likely to cause injury, or that it was acceptable within the level that has already been established, so he lets it go.

He doesn't forget it, though. He might think to himself, 'Okay, that was a hook. That's okay, but if there's too many then I'll have to start to call them.' Then there is another hook. The referee makes a note again, maybe it wasn't any more severe, but perhaps thinking that if the guy does it a third time then he'll have to call it. Then comes the retaliation. That might be the point where enough is enough, so he calls it. (He will probably also decide to backtrack a little and call the second hook as well, even though at the time he wouldn't have, so that neither team gets a powerplay. The fans still think he's inconsistent, though, because one guy hooked twice, and one only once, but both got the same punishment.) He might also call the third hook because when players retaliate it suggests that the level of the game is getting too high, and needs to be calmed down. This is one of the reasons why retaliatory penalties tend to be called more often than instigating ones. The initial hook might have been just a misjudged action in the heat of the moment. The retaliatory hook though, is in response to that, and there is intent there. To prevent the game escalating, where it can get dangerous for players, the final one has to be called. Fans and players often get upset by this, because they think the referee is seeing one player foul but not the other, when in fact he is seeing both players foul, but using his judgement as to whether or not to call them. Of course, he may get it right, he may get it wrong, but if he calls all of them then he is accused of not letting the game flow, and if he doesn't call them then someone could get hurt. Catch 22.

Sometimes, though, the retaliatory penalty gets called and the instigating one doesn't. This may simply be because instigating penalties tend to be perpetrated more subtly. A ref might not be able to see a defender slyly grabbing an attacker, but it's a bit more obvious when the attacker then turns round and wraps his stick around the defender's head. 'Sometimes, you don't see what started it. That's the problem,' concedes Kirkham. 'It can be either behind your back, or say there's a mêlée of players in front of you and sometimes you can't actually see why something started. If you get a clear view then you can give both – you've got to give the two, there's no way you can just give the one – but you can try and give the guy who started it an extra minor penalty. Then that gives a signal to the players that you're watching them.'

One of the things that has made it more difficult for referees in recent years has been the improvement in the standard of hockey, and with it, the increase in speed. 'The refereeing has improved,' says Ron Shudra, when I asked him how the refereeing in the Superleague compared to the old Heineken days. 'But there's still room for improvement. It wasn't terrible refereeing. I mean it was good for the standard that was there. But I think the league has outgrown the standard of the refereeing right now. The referees have improved tenfold – but the game's improved twentyfold. The league is a lot more competitive. There's a lot more going on all through the games and it's quicker. Guys have improved and so referees have to be a little bit smarter.'

Partly the increased demands on the referees are down to the sheer pace of the game now. 'A lot of it comes down to fitness,' says Kirkham, 'because that can play a major part. If you're unfit, or tired, there's no way you can call the game the same way you did at the start. Your level goes down. Concentration, and skating. Things are a lot quicker now. You have to know how to pace yourself. I think the league has gone up since I first started doing Premier Division hockey. Really, it is out of sight compared to what it was then. But also, the pressures on the referee have gone out of sight as well. I'm not saying we can't do it, because I know we can, but the pressure now is greater.'

There remains though, the strong feeling that referees are inconsistent. Particularly, when you start to compare refs from other countries. Kirkham, though, doesn't feel that this is the case. Although it might not appear that way to us at times, Kirkham feels that referees will nearly always agree when there has been an infraction. 'We do have seminars, and we do have people talking to us. I've been in IIHF seminars, with the top referees in the world, and spoken to them about it. And all the referees roughly see everything the same way. Perhaps we don't *call* it the same way, but we *see* it the same way. I've worked with Germans, Austrians, Czechs, Russians, and there's not that much difference in the way we see things.' Perhaps refs aren't as inconsistent as they seem. The rules are interpreted the same way by the refs, it is just the level of the game, the line, that is set differently. What is tolerated, and what is not. That is always going to be difficult to judge, because it depends on the ref's intuitive understanding and feel for the game. Interestingly, for those of us who think of North American hockey as being more violent than our own game, it seems players are given a little more leeway here. 'In Canada and in America they do call it a lot stricter than they do here,' says Kirkham. 'I know Canadian refs who've said to me that they call it a lot, lot tighter. There are a few things they do here that they wouldn't get away with over there.'

Of course, sometimes the refs have strict guidelines laid down on what they should and shouldn't allow. One of the most contentious areas, and certainly one which you do see called differently from country to country, concerns fighting. As someone who has played the game, and been a part of it for so long, Kirkham is able to accept it, within reason. 'With speed being such a feature of the game, fighting is part and parcel of it. Though you have to draw the line. I don't like people using sticks as any kind of weapon, for instance. I've never seen anyone hurt in a fight. A few black eyes, bruises maybe, but I have seen people hurt by sticks. That's where I draw the line. I think, as a ref, that's a no-no. That's so dangerous. Keep sticks below the shoulder. You ask any players and they'll agree. Of course, you don't always see it. You have to realise players are watching you, seeing where you are, and when your back is turned the sticks can go in. They're not stupid. They know you'll throw them out if you see it. You can't always see it.'

Fights also have to be judged in the context of the game. Some referees might throw players out of a game at the first sign of fighting, but Kirkham tends to take a more lenient view. He cites an example: 'I was doing a game at Ayr, and there were a couple of guys, you know, handbags at dawn, and so I gave them two minutes each. Then it happened again, so I gave them two plus two, and said, "I don't want any more. The fans have had a bit of a spectacle. They've seen a bit of rough stuff between you. You've each given a bit, and taken some. But any more and you're out the game." It then went off *again* so they got five plus game and were kicked out. There wasn't any more fighting after that. That's the level. That's the line, and it's been stepped over.' Whilst the *Daily Mail* would no doubt think it was deplorable that an official should tolerate such disgraceful scenes, there is also the argument that fights can act as a safety valve. If there is no release for any of the tension that can build up during a game, players are more likely to resort to using their sticks to get even. A fight can help clear the air.

Sometimes though, a players' feud can carry on not only throughout a game, but over the course of several games, or even, as in the celebrated case of Messrs Ruggles and Kummu, over the course of several years. What does a referee do when he has two guys on the ice whom he knows will eventually end up going for each other? Do repeat offenders get special attention? Surprisingly, perhaps, the answer is no. 'I might keep my eye on them, but I won't treat them any differently,' says Kirkham. 'If they start I'll say, "Okay guys, if you want to drop the gloves and have a go, then go ahead – but don't expect me to bale you out."'

This brings us to another part of the referee's job – the saver of face. As anyone who has seen a few hockey fights will know, these contests have their own rules and etiquette. Occasionally, two players will go head to toe and slug it out. Venting their frustrations, they'll really tear into each other, and at the end, bruised and breathless, they may even have established a level of respect for each other in the process. More often, however, no actual fighting takes place. Sometimes, players drop the gloves, circle around each other a few times, make with the 'come on' gestures, and then, once they are safely separated from each other by teammates and officials, they can start giving it some serious lip. Other times, they'll quickly lunge at each other, grab hold of each other's sweaters so that no actual punching can take place, and then grimly hang onto each other until the ref arrives to split them up and escort them to the safety of the penalty box. (Erm, except in the case of Ruggles versus Kummu, where Kummu might then follow Ruggles into the box and lay into him from there . . .)

Sometimes, however, one of the guys concerned will be a madman, and there will be a very real danger that his opponent may be about to lose some teeth. In this case, the correct etiquette is for the weaker man to skate around backwards, waving his puny fists and saying to his opponent 'Come on then, do you want some?' whilst trying to catch the eye of the official who can then leap in and save him and hopefully prevent a humiliating pummelling. This kind of brinkmanship is all too familiar to Kirkham. As is 'The Look'. This is the facial expression used by players who want the ref to please come in now and my god look at the size of him please stop this now I want my mum. 'I could name you players that do that,' laughs Kirkham, who sadly, in the interests of good player/referee relations, then doesn't.

'Say someone picks on Mike Ware, and they are pushing and shoving, but then it starts to get a bit serious, then it's a case of "Quick, I don't want to go any more!" You can see it in their face, and the look in their eyes of pure . . . fear. That somebody is going to beat the shit out of them – and they've started it! "Oh please help me." I've seen it time and time again. And me and the linesmen will have a good laugh about it later. "Did you see his face? It was a picture." Sometimes, in the heat of play, they start on someone without really seeing who it is. And then they realise who it is they've picked on. Then they go "Aargh! Please, someone help me." So then you step in . . . ' But surely, I thought, you must be tempted, every now and then, to think, 'Hmm, I'll just let this run a little. See what happens . . . ' Kirkham's response is slightly sheepish. 'Ah, well . . . Yeah, that does happen. (Laughs) We're like elephants; we don't forget. You've got a guy who's been winding you up all night . . . I mean why not? We're only human! They've started it. "Well, we'll just see what develops." Then you step in. Eventually.' If moments

Jeff Jablonski, EHL game,
Manchester 1997

Panthers v. Steelers, Championship final 1997

Storm fan, 1997

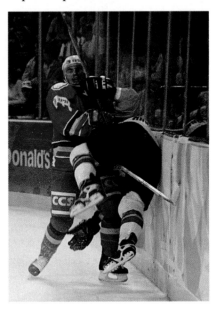

Uncomfortable moment for Craig
Woodcroft, 1997

Storm v. Steelers, 1997

Sheffield cheerleaders, 1994

Steelers fans, 1994

The national anthem, Manchester 1997

Warm up, Sheffield 1994

Sheffield Arena, 1994

Face-off, Panthers v. Steelers, 1997

Kurt Kleinendorst in a reflective mood, 1997

Steelers v. Milton Keynes Kings, 1994

MC Jon Hammond   Young fan, Manchester 1997

Storm v. Steelers, 1997

like this are among the most gratifying for an official – when suddenly, the guy who all evening long has been saying what an asshole he thinks you are, now wants to be your very best friend – then it should be remembered that the referee himself often gets hurt too.

It is, of course, one of those fantastic moments in hockey. A split second of action that you know you'll never forget. The referee getting hit by the puck. What a simple joy that is. I remember it happening once at the Nynex whilst I was drinking a coke and finding it so funny that I laughed some through my nose. Tell me, Simon, how does that feel? 'It bloody hurts,' he began, prompting an uneasy pang of guilt for me as he continued. 'We're called puck magnets. When you do a game and you know you're the puck magnet there's nothing you can do to get out of the way of the puck. I've been hit in the face, in the mouth, in the back of the head. We never used to wear helmets, four or five years ago – a bit of bravado, I suppose – and I can remember once being a linesman and the puck came round the back of the goal. A shot rapped off the plexi, and I ducked, but the puck hit me on the back of the head. The whistle blew, with me rolling around the boards with blood pouring down the back of my head, and all I got was Todd Bidner moaning "I was on a breakaway and you blew the whistle!" I said, "Thanks Todd."'

Now that I had established that refs were human too, I wondered if, like the players, they got more fired up for particular games. 'I try and treat every game the same. I think it would be wrong to call a game any differently from what it had been during the season. I think I would be wrong setting myself up that way. Okay, so sometimes you step on the ice and there's 17,000 people there, and you feel a bit differently from the way you would if there were 1,000 people there, but you try and call it the same.' But having said that, Kirkham did admit that it was special to oversee a final. One year was particularly special to him – the 1996 Wembley Championships – when as a stand-in he was called upon to run the second semi-final whilst still recovering from refereeing the first. 'I've had the unique advantage of refereeing all three games at Wembley, two semis and the final. But, I'll tell you, I enjoyed that weekend so much. John Moore got injured. The only trouble then was I was going into a game where you have to follow the level set by someone else, which I hopefully did, but that is difficult sometimes.'

It's easy to forget that, although he may sometimes look like the loneliest guy on the planet, the referee does have some help out there. How important is the relationship between a ref and his two linesmen? 'I think it's a very important relationship. We are like the third team on the ice. A good linesman will anticipate the play. Be there on a breakaway, or be there if a scuffle breaks out. That can always stop things getting serious. You have to be there for them, and you rely on them. You have to be in tune with each other. You know each other's strengths and weaknesses. And you have to protect your linesmen from players sometimes. I don't like my linesmen taking too much abuse.'

However hard Kirkham and his colleagues work at getting things right on the ice, some people are always going to be unshaken in their belief that referees in this country are rubbish. To improve the standard of refereeing, they argue, we should bring in more top officials from Canada. Kirkham's response to this specious reasoning is blunt: 'What top officials from Canada?' Anyone who has followed the game in North America would be aware that NHL referees are amongst the most vilified in the world. According to fans and players, they are rubbish. 'Nowhere in the world is there a good referee, apparently,' muses Kirkham. 'Besides, there's the work permit issue. How many of them would even be allowed to work here? And anyway, once they'd been here a while they'd be calling the game the same as us anyway, so what's the point?

'It doesn't annoy me, but I'd like to say, "Okay, guys. You pick any country in Europe and then pick a referee. Within two weeks, or a month, you'll hate them as much as you hate us . . ." That includes the fans and the players. So what do you want, the devil you know or the devil you don't know? Because the devil you don't know is going to come in and you're going to say, "Great. He's marvellous isn't he?" Then within two months . . . they've all had it. You can ask Kyle Smart, you can ask Mike Rowe. When they start they are the best thing since sliced bread. Then all of a sudden, a game happens where they have to start calling a lot of penalties, and major penalties. Not through their fault – because they never wield the stick, or start the fight – but because of the actions of the players, and they have to call big penalties. And you're always going to piss someone off when you do that. That's always going to be the case. I mean you can get the best referee in the world, you can get (Andy) Van Hellemond over here. For the first couple of months you'll think he's brilliant. Because of the respect he's got. But then he'll have to make the tight call in a big game, and something will happen and there you go. He's a mere mortal like the rest of us.'

Surely, though, fans continue to moan, something could be done to improve referees. What about video evidence? Whilst he doesn't feel they would make as much difference to games as some people think, Kirkham is not entirely averse to the idea. 'Goal judges can miss things, I've known guys talking to their mates miss things. In some instances it might be nice to say, "Was that a goal? Can we see it again?" but no-one's got the facilities. Unless, maybe, you are doing a Sky game, and then you can see replays. They have the camera in the goal, but even then that doesn't always show things clearly.' But do we need video replays? 'Personally, I think no. There's not that many goals you are uncertain of. You can count them on one hand. You could argue for ever, of course, but with the guys we have in the league I don't think we need it. I don't think they would pay for it to be set up anyway.'

In the NHL, where cost is not so much of an issue, they have got video facilities, and, at the time of writing, fans are complaining about the length of time it is taking for officials to review incidents on video. Whereas before, an official would have made the call in an instant, they are now deferring to video judges for fear of being contradicted or proved wrong. This has caused so many interminable delays, without seeming to have improved the quality of the calls anyway, that fans are now calling for the whole thing to be scrapped. With so many stoppages, games are no longer flowing, and the benefits of using video evidence have been outweighed by the fact that referees are less inclined to trust their own judgement and, ironically, are making more mistakes as a result. However, in the never-ending quest for refereeing perfection the NHL are also putting around the idea of utilising two referees. Kirkham is not impressed.

'No. I can't see it. You're out there on your own. You're the guy that's setting the level of the penalties. But if there's two of you, you can't do it if one guy calls everything, whilst one guy calls nothing. You can't do it. Two guys, both know the rules, tripping, hooking, etc, but one guy may let it go because there's no animosity, but the other guy wants to call it tighter. What if you see something in the other guy's end, that he's missed, can you overrule him? How would that work? I understand the logic behind it, of wanting it, but the logistics mean I can't see it working.'

Another area in which refereeing is being brought into question is when players are disciplined or fined by the league after a game in which, at the time, the referee didn't call anything. I wondered if Kirkham felt the league was undermining referees when they did this. 'No. Not at all. We may have missed it, or not seen an incident. Personally, I don't mind it. I have no problems with the idea. Maybe they should tell players they are going to do it. That in itself would be a deterrent. But we don't get to see any post-game videos, so it's hard for us to comment. It's taken out of our hands. It's nothing to do with us. It's the ISL. I give what I see. If, after that, further action is taken, then that's up to them. I have no jurisdiction, and I don't really want any. I call it as I see it, on the ice, in that split second. Not with hindsight.'

And yet, even with discipline committees, and video cameras and talk of import refs, people still seem convinced that something needs to be done about the way games are handled. Perhaps the only real solution to the problem is to not even see it as a problem in the first place. It is an impossible job. Mistakes will be made. If you accept that referees are giving it their best effort, which most people do, then where is the problem? No one ever blames a player when they know he has done the best he can, so why blame a ref in the same situation? It is the same for both sides. For his part, and despite the barrage of criticism that is continually hurled at him by disgruntled observers, there is actually very little about the way the game is handled that Kirkham himself would actually alter. 'Out of the whole of a season, there's not much you would change.' True, referees sometimes get it wrong, but it is not as if they are continually going against certain teams or players. Kirkham is able to see the bigger picture. 'It goes both ways, and at the end of a season, it comes out in the middle. It swings both ways. For and against. Perhaps that's not the way to look at it, but that's the way it works. And most people would say they could live with it. We just call the game as we see it. That's all we can do.'

And so, oddly, I find myself agreeing. After speaking to Kirkham, I found that I started to view the game differently. I took a more lenient view towards refs. It is quite an eye-opening experience to sit down and watch a game and try and discipline yourself into accepting the ref is always right. It's hard to do because, obviously, he isn't right all the time, but if you give it a go you'll be surprised to learn that he's right far more often than you thought he was going to be. Sit back and watch your fellow fans. Watch the way their eyes bulge with apoplectic rage as their team is penalised. Listen to the abuse poured down on the referee. Then think how you would have viewed the incident if you supported the other team. Suddenly, everything isn't so black and white any more. Suddenly, there is a lot of grey in there. You can't really get as worked up yourself, to be so indignant at this apparent malfeasance, because you can see the other side of the argument. Much as I am naturally averse to sticking up for authority figures, I do sympathise with the referees. We treat them like scum, and I know it sounds trite, but without them there would be no game in the first place. We blame them for everything, so that less of the blame might fall on our own team. ('We'd have won that, if it wasn't for the ref!' snarl the fans.) The next time your team loses you can blame it all on the ref, if you like, after all, you won't be the only one doing it, but ask yourself, who are you really kidding? It's time to change the record.

Rocket Man

If, by some chance, you ever find yourself with a few spare million quid tucked down the back of your sofa and shrewdly you decide that the most efficient way to benefit mankind with these riches is to launch a new ice hockey franchise, you might start to wonder who the first player you're going to sign will be. Obviously, it's a tricky one. It would have to be someone dependable and committed, with as much presence off the ice as on it, someone you could build the entire franchise around. If, Frankenstein style, you could build yourself some kind of hockey monster, you might want to consider plundering various attributes from the world's best. Your creature could have the behemothic stature of Eric Lindros, be able to snap pucks through fridge doors like Brett Hull, would have the hockey brain of Wayne Gretzky, the bewitching skills of Mario Lemieux and the formidable leadership qualities of Mark Messier. Why, such a player would be not so much a man, but a god. A colossus on whose shoulders you could hang the fate of your entire club. Mind you, it does sound like a lot of tedious mucking about. It would probably be a lot easier just to give Ron Shudra a call instead. He's no god, but he'd do the job just as well. Just ask the Sheffield Steelers.

Ron Shudra was born in Winnipeg in 1967 – though he played the bulk of his junior hockey around Edmonton, Alberta. A talented and hard working defenceman, he was drafted by the Oilers in 1986 who, spookily, that year also plumped for Kim Issel, Ivan Matulik and Tony Hand, familiar names to British fans. Like most kids in his position, it was an intoxicating position to be in. Shudra remembers being thrilled by it, even if it didn't mean instant stardom. 'Like anybody, you're 17 or 18 years old, and you're just happy to get drafted by anybody.' He remembers: 'I was fortunate enough to get drafted, I was Edmonton's third pick, 63rd overall. You're happy to get picked, obviously. You go to camp, they're looking at you to develop a little bit, and play here and there. First year it didn't work out. Obviously I was still 18 years old. No one expects you to make it – even the first overalls, they aren't always expected to make it right away. I got sent back to junior – I was one of the last guys cut, to Kamloops, to play another year of junior.'

Back in juniors, the coaching staff saw the potential in him to be used as a utility player. Accustomed as British fans are to seeing him patrolling the blueline, he was to finish that first year with the Kamloops Blazers, of the WHL, playing right wing, rather than defence. 'I got drafted as a defenceman. I went to the main camp in Edmonton, played a few exhibition games, went back to the juniors, and they asked the coach, who was then Ken Hitchcock, (now head honcho with the Dallas Stars) if they could try me at wing. So I tried that, fine. They kept me up on wing. The next year at camp I played a little bit of both. Then, instead of being sent back to junior, because of my birthday – I was going to turn 20 during the season, and you had to be 20 to play in the American Hockey League – they sent me to Halifax in the American League.'

It was his first real year in pro hockey, and a few months into it he got called up by the Oilers and managed to grab ten NHL games, playing half the games as a forward, and half as a defenceman, picking up five assists along the way. Most Canadian kids could have died happy, right there and then. He had realised his dream of making it to the NHL. Obviously, this would have been pretty special under any circumstances, but the Edmonton Oilers at that time were an exceptional side – arguably the best hockey club of the modern era. The season

Shudra made the team, they were coming off the back of a Stanley Cup win, their third in four years, and later that year they would make it four out of five when they swept the Boston Bruins aside 4–0. People were already talking about them as a dynasty – like the TV show only with more stars. Among the names on that roster were (take a deep breath) Glen Anderson, Geoff Courtnall, Grant Fuhr, Jari Kurri, Kevin Lowe, Mark Messier, Andy Moog, Marty McSorly, Esa Tikkanen and the big G himself, Wayne Gretzky. That's *Wayne Gretzky*. Stick anyone of those ten on a Superleague team and you'd probably win the league, even now, a decade on – they were that good. If it had been me thrown into that team, I would have cacked myself.

It was pretty scary for Shudra too. 'No kidding. With all the guys they had on their team . . . ' So what was it like, I wondered, being thrown into a side like that at such a young age? Intimidating, or what? 'The guys were pretty good. I mean, they've all been there before. They don't treat you any different. They don't treat you as some kid. They respect you for being there. And you respect them for being there as well. There were a few guys that were a little more difficult to talk to than others, but in general they were very enthusiastic and helped me out in any way they could.' Surely, though, he must have been a bit star struck. 'Sure you were,' admits Shudra, who like many seasoned professional athletes, has a tendency to talk in the second person. 'You go up and it's like "Holy cow". All of a sudden you're in a dressing room with guys you've been watching on TV. They were big names then – they're still big names now. You'd sit beside one of them, and turn to one side and you'd got Mark Messier there. Turn to the other side and you'd got Kevin Lowe on the other side. You look across and you're staring at Wayne Gretzky. You know, it's kind of . . . ' He paused a moment, looking for the right way to express the impact it had on him. 'You open your eyes in a hurry. But like I said, they were very good guys, and they helped out as much as they could.'

I could tell Shudra could anticipate my next question. Fleetingly embarrassed at being about to ask such an inane, no-brainer, I decided it was best to get it out the way early on so we could both get on with the rest of our lives. So, Wayne Gretzky then, um, ha . . . *What's he like?* I could tell I wasn't the first person to mention the G word to Ron. 'People always want to know what he was like,' says Shudra, without any noticeable irritation. 'To me, he was quiet in the dressing room. He wasn't one that would yell and scream and shout. He was a quiet leader, motivator sort of thing. He led by example, whereas the guys that spoke a little more were Messier and Kevin Lowe. Marty McSorley – he was very surprising. He was a good team player. A good team motivator. Very intense guy when he wanted to be and very happy-go-lucky when he didn't want to be. They all fit together very well.'

Despite being in such illustrious company, Shudra doesn't recall any feelings of not belonging there. 'You worked hard enough to get noticed on the farm team to be brought up, so you must have been doing something right.' But the reality of his situation was that he was but a bit player on a team of superstars. At that time, it took an exceptional mix of players to win the Stanley Cup, the chemistry had to be exactly right, and only three teams had managed it in 13 seasons. It would have to be a hell of a player to disturb the alchemy. On another team, in a different time, he would have had a solid chance, but there he was never likely to be able to carve out a place for himself – not on *that* team. The next year he went along to training camp again, and again was sent back to Halifax. From there he was shipped to another of the farm teams, the Cape Breton Oilers. Then Edmonton decided to trade his rights to the New York Rangers, which meant he now had to up and move sticks to the Rangers' farm team in Denver, Fort Wayne. But by now it was more a case of forget Wayne. Shudra realised that he was likely to be facing a career in the minors. He had had a taste of the big league and NHL stardom, but if it was going to happen to him at all, it would, in all likelihood have happened by now. Then, in 1990, a call from England provided an unexpected opportunity for something completely different.

Even the most loyal Barons fan would have conceded that

there is a bit of a difference between the legendary Edmonton Coliseum and the Hobs Moat Road, in Solihull. With all due respect, the place is a depressing, dirty, abhorrent dump – though I might be romanticising it a little. Yet in just a few short months, Ron Shudra had gone from being an Oiler to being, well, just being oily. He had signed for the Solihull Barons. Even allowing for the fact that at the time they were a Premier Division outfit, this still seems an odd career move. 'Well like anything, it was an opportunity to try something different,' says Shudra, diplomatically. 'I just thought that maybe I'd have more of a chance of playing over here rather than being yanked up and down, and being pushed all over the country back home.' Okay, so it was understandable wanting to try out England, but why Solihull, of all places? 'Solihull had phoned my agent, said they were looking for players. My agent just said, "Well, what do you think? Do you feel like you want to try this or do you want to stay here?"' It was obviously a big decision. One that would shape his entire life. 'I just said, "Whatever. Whatever you think's good."'

And so, trusting to fate, Shudra arrived in the Midlands. Presumably, he didn't really know what he was getting into – he'd just signed for Solihull, how clued up could he have been? So what were his first impressions? (long pause) 'You don't know what to expect, obviously, when you come in. You walk in the building, and go, "Urgh, this is kind of a dreary place . . . " – which is true, I mean, it is. But it does have a lot of character in it, if you look at it that way. I mean, the people then that were going to the games were – you pretty much knew everybody. And we were getting decent crowds back then.' In fairness to the Barons, the support was always the best thing about the team. A vociferous bunch, they took to Shudra from the off, though for his part, the actual playing side took a little getting used to.

'The league itself, you know, you come in on a Thursday, practise once, and go to Humberside and get beaten 18–3, you play 55 minutes, and it's kind of "What the heck did I stumble on to here?"' Still, if more ice time was what he had been after, then he was in the right place. 'I was playing all the time, that's for sure. It was very, very difficult to adjust, the first little while. To play, you know, 40 minutes plus, a game. Once the season got to Christmas, though, you got used to it and 40, 50, 60 minutes, it was easy – well, it wasn't *easy*, but you knew how to pace yourself to last the 60 minutes. Whether it would be making a rush, then taking time off to play in defence, and then making a couple of rushes, and you know, taking a couple of penalties.'

Nevertheless, he could have been forgiven for having second thoughts. 'Sure, you second-guess it a little bit,' he admits, 'but you stick it out and try and work the best you can. Once you get over that initial couple of weeks' period you concentrate on the game and do the best you can.' Even so, how many guys in his position would have stuck out playing in a league so obviously below what they were capable of playing in, and so soon after experiencing life at the most celebrated hockey club in the world? Most guys would have sacked it. Not our Ron. 'I'm not really that type of person, that's the thing. I mean it's been done before, guys coming in to Durham – remember? Guys flew over, saw the building, then flew back the next day! And that happened to them a few times in the past. But I'm not that type of person. If I find something I try and stick with it for as long as I can, or as long as they want me to.'

Perhaps surprisingly, once he got a bit more accustomed to the way things were in Britain, and started to get to grips with it, he happily threw himself into what he saw as a new challenge. Pretty soon, he was starting to have some fun. 'I did. I enjoyed it, yeah,' he recalls, although he admits a few adjustments had to be made. 'I mean you have to learn how to play the game a little more smartly. You have to work your angles a little more. You have to know when to exert yourself, and when to conserve some energy. Plus it also develops your mental skills a little bit, and your physical skills. When you're out there and you're tired, you have to think a little bit more, and try and play a little bit smarter. And your physical skills too, well, to handle the puck a little better in different situations. I mean I could handle the puck when I came over, but I think I can do it better now than what I could before.'

Surprisingly, for someone who had shared a locker room with the Great One, Shudra started to find that he was a better player in Solihull than he had been in Edmonton. He was being asked to do a hell of a lot more, for a start, and he was thriving on the challenge. 'If you think about it, the more you play at a game level the better you're gonna get,' he says, simply. 'That's what it basically was. We only practised twice a week, and we played twice a week but I would play all through those games. So you had to drag your skills up kicking and screaming 'cos that's what it took.' He was certainly under no illusions about the task ahead of his team. Even before he had arrived, there had been a few setbacks at the Moat.

Initially, Jim Lynch had been pencilled in to coach the team, but unhappy with aspects of the club's management, he had pulled out at short notice, leaving the club with just four senior players signed up. It was left to a certain inexperienced team manager called Dave Simms to frantically try and patch things up, and even when Shudra arrived to shore up a defence that had been as watertight as a burst colander, the results at first were pretty dire. Realising that change had to be made, the Barons sacked coach Gary Fay and looked towards Shudra for more help. 'Around Christmas time they fired the coach, or should I say relieved him of his job, and Brent Sapergia [import player-coach] and I took over.' The emergency surgery was to do the trick. Between them, the two players slowly turned things around, and Shudra, though still only in his early 20s himself, was asked to draw on his experiences in Canada to help lead the team.

'Brent and I were passing stuff along. Obviously, he had played a few more years professionally than I had, but we both had that professional background of being taught by some of the best coaches, and we just passed it on to the players. You had to look at the team we had then. There were a lot of younger guys who were basically just 17, 18 years old, and who just went out and ran around like crazy. That was the way it was for a lot of teams. They'd have six guys who played all the time, and then the rest would be a bunch of kids. As long as you could teach the kids not to get scored upon by the other kids, then hopefully your imports would cancel each other out.' With a lot of hard work, the team did manage to put a few results together, and scrambled just clear of the relegation zone at season's end.

'We were actually very successful the last half of the year,' Shudra recalls with some satisfaction. 'We won 13 of 17 games or something, whereas before Christmas we had only won about three games . . . ' For a young player, Shudra's initiation into the world of coaching had been pretty daunting, though at least he had enjoyed the full support of the players. 'I mean the guys there wanted to learn a little bit, and they were very enthusiastic and they wanted to better themselves in the game, and it didn't take much.' Wisely, Shudra had thought it best not to get too technical with his charges. 'It was very simple, it was like "Well, you go here, you go there. And if it changes, then you go here, you go there . . . that's all you have to do."'

Although they were both working their butts off trying to keep the club going, Shudra and Sapergia weren't the only ones making a contribution. 'We had a couple of British guys who were decent forwards as well,' Shudra recalls. 'Ronnie Wood was good in his day, Jim Pennycook was okay in his day, Stewart Parker, you know, these guys could still score goals and put the puck in the net. We had a few guys on defence, Phil Lee and Perry Doyle, who was young and used to run around like crazy. Once you could control them a little bit, and just teach them that . . . you don't have to go in there and run someone and put him into next week. Go in there, take the body, finish the check. That's all you got to do, then get out. We'd try to get the point across, how to forecheck, how to backcheck. Just little things that the young kids would say "Oh gee, maybe that'll work . . ." You know, put a lightbulb in their head . . . '

The image of Shudra that comes across at this time is one of a 40-year-old guy helplessly trapped inside the body of a 23-year-old. Feeling that his responsibility to his teammates extended beyond the rink, there was no question of him shirking his parental duties. 'Brent and I, we were the kind of guys that would have the guys over after a game as well. We'd chat with them, and have a drink with them, or whatever. So it was one of those things where you were still part of the team. You weren't trying to put yourself above anybody. You'd say, come on boys, come on back to my house, we'll have some drinks and some eats, chat about whatever. And it turned out that every week we'd do that.' It wasn't how he had planned things at the start, but he was comfortable with the role. 'At the beginning of the year you're just trying to fit in and keep a pretty low profile, but that's hard to do when you're an import 'cos they don't expect that. There was a lot of pressure back then on imports. If you didn't perform, or didn't score, then they got rid of you. I mean, we got through 11 imports that year. I think that's why so many teams were having trouble with money because they were flying guys in left, right and centre.'

With so many guys trying their hands at this playing in Britain lark, and so many failing, the life expectancy for imports was increasingly comparable to that of an 18-year-old Kansas conscript engaging the Viet Cong on his first tour of duty. One of the reasons for this, Shudra thinks, wasn't that they weren't good enough, but because of the type of player they were. 'Some guys weren't individually talented players. They were team talented, where if they had someone to give them the puck they could score goals.' This wasn't what was called for. 'You had to be able to do everything well.' The kind of player who would succeed in Britain at that time wasn't so much a guy who could slot into a team, but a guy who could carry one.

It's fair to say that the Barons had a mixed start to their next season. After eight games in the Autumn Cup, which they managed to complete without too much embarrassment to themselves, they were then the subject of a takeover bid by the newly formed Sheffield Steelers, who wanted to buy the club so as to gain access to the Premier Division. When this move was ruled out by the BIHA – who had the tendency to make the Luddites look like a group of radical, forward-thinking visionaries – the Steelers were forced to begin life in the English League, and the Barons, suddenly without the cash bond needed to preserve their Premier Division status, tumbled down a couple of leagues overnight to join them. The Steelers' general manager job went to the Baron's player Ronnie Wood, and he was quick to lure Shudra along with him. Not that it took a lot of arm twisting. 'I drove up, saw the building and said "Okay",' Shudra recalls. It was fair to say that the brand new 8,500 capacity Sheffield Arena was a more impressive venue than Hobs Moat.

'The facility was great to see, and to play in. To have that as a home rink, it was great. Considering some of the places you could play at that time,' admits Shudra. His role on the team, as at Solihull, was to extend beyond merely playing. With so many seats to fill, the Steelers had to look to a new audience to sell the game to, and Shudra was happy to do what he could to help out. 'You could see the possibilities – that you had to help get the team going, to do some promotional work.' And so Shudra was sent out to meet the people of Sheffield to help promote the game. Coming from a country where hockey is the religion, to one where it was a curiosity, must have been pretty difficult for many players but, fortunately for the Steelers, Shudra was the perfect guy to have on board at that time. Intelligent, congenial and hard-working, he threw himself into the cause without compunction. 'That's just the way I am. I saw a challenge, went to work, and tried to do the best I could,' he says, matter-of-factly. 'We were out there trying to build the sport. So you have to go out and put on a certain personality, let yourself go in certain ways. So we did.' One of the ways he did this was simply to always seem accessible. Naturally affable anyway, he just let himself go with the flow. 'We tried to be approachable,' he remembers. 'People identified with you. They'd come and talk to you. They couldn't even approach footballers. You just don't. They are not approachable people. We worked hard to sell the sport as a family game and people responded.'

For the first few months, Shudra's entire life was taken up by the Steelers. 'Ronnie Wood and I brought Stevie Nemeth in.

And the three of us would work in the office every day from eight in the morning to eight at night, trying to get things right, and get things working. Ronnie and I were commuting from Birmingham at one point, for the first month and a half. So we were leaving at about seven, and not getting back till nine at night.

'We got in the best players we could for the money we had. Guys that we knew would be personality-friendly, I guess. And it worked. It snowballed.' The Steelers were a success almost from the off. To the astonishment of those who said they'd never do it, they managed to sell out the building in their very first season. Shudra enjoyed proving the doubters wrong. 'I think a lot of people weren't ready for that style of hockey to come out. They were still in the "olden days", let's say. They were still thinking the way they had been for 15 years.' Shudra's philosophy was that anything that helped grab people's attention was worth trying. 'You gotta get them hooked somehow. We got them hooked.' And he had loved every moment of it. 'It was a lot of fun being behind the scenes and getting into everything. Trying to get it to the level it is. And you could see it pay off with the way the crowd was. From Christmas onwards you couldn't buy a ticket in Sheffield. They were sold out every game. Even we couldn't get them. Everything sold out. We were going "Holy Cow"'cos we didn't expect things to go that fast. We were probably overwhelmed a little in the back rooms.'

If the amount of hard work that Shudra was putting in off the ice seemed prodigious, it should be remembered that he was playing too – so at least he was getting a couple of hours of decent rest every week. After getting to grips with Premier Division hockey the year before, the drop down a couple of leagues was hardly likely to push Shudra to the limit. 'To me it was fairly easy,' he admits. 'But again, we were playing 60 minutes, and coaching, and working hard,' he adds, as if afraid to give the impression he had slacked at all. Exciting though those early days with the Steelers must have been, surely Shudra must have had reservations about playing in a league as modest as the English League. 'My dad was more worried about it than I was. He said, "What do you want to drop down there for?" I said, "Well, it's an opportunity. We don't plan on being there that long, we're going to try and get up into the next division, then the next division after that."' True to the script, the Steelers mauled most of the opposition thrown in their path and clinched promotion to the First Division in their debut season, and the year after, did it again to gain access to the Premier.

By now, the Steelers were becoming a more formidable outfit all round. For the first year and a half, coaching duties had been shared between Shudra and Nemeth, but in the second year Alex Dampier came on board as head coach allowing Shudra to once again concentrate on playing. Shudra admits it was a weight off his shoulders. 'Oh sure. It's very difficult to play and coach at the same time. You can't see everything that's happening at the time, and it's a little easier when there's someone on the bench. You don't want to come off on a shift and be tired and then have to yell at someone for something you saw before, and still play. It just makes it difficult when you have to do both.'

It is also more difficult for teammates to deal with a player when he is also their coach. On a personal level, it is better for players to get along with each other, so that some of that closeness and spirit can translate itself in to the play. A coach will generally have to be a little bit more detached and aloof, so that he can make decisions about his team without his personal feelings interfering. Unless a player-coach happens to be schizophrenic, he's going to find combining both jobs a bit tricky. 'You really have to work hard at separating the playing from the coaching,' Shudra feels. 'And players have to know that when you're doing one thing you're doing it as a coach, and when you do another thing it's as a player. It's totally different.' There was also a problem when it was Shudra himself who had made a mistake as a player. 'Exactly. I mean what do you do when you know *you've* made the mistake. Do you yell at yourself?'

Fortunately for Shudra, life was to become much simpler.

After never spending more than a couple of seasons with any particular side, and rarely having the same role, or playing the same position, Shudra started to make himself feel at home in Sheffield, and at the time of writing, he had been with the Steelers for each of their seven seasons. Though he's happy with the way things have panned out, it was obviously never something he had planned on. 'Well true. Obviously you want to stay somewhere like here as long as you can. You want to do that because you get to know the city, and meet the people, and you start to feel comfortable. You don't want to get *too* comfortable. You still want to be able to perform. You want to still have challenges.' Well, he was obviously in the right place there, then.

As the Steelers made their way up through the leagues, and the standard of hockey around them rose, so Shudra was faced with fresh challenges every season. Generally, they were met. After winning promotion in each of their first two seasons, they were runners-up in their first season in the top flight, won the league and Championship double the year after, and then were so greedy that a Grand Slam followed in the 1995/96 season. After gorging himself on so much silverware, you might think that Shudra would start to look for fresh challenges elsewhere, but he refutes any suggestion that he has achieved everything he wants to in Sheffield. 'It still doesn't mean I don't have goals. I still want to win championships. I still want to see the European League. A proper league with interlocking schedule. They do it in North America.'

Of course, a few years earlier, this sort of thing would have sounded rather fanciful, but the success of the Steelers in paving the way for arena hockey in Britain, coupled with the massive jump in playing standards and the advent of the Superleague means that Shudra's ambitions don't sound so far-fetched now. In fact, whilst I am reluctant to try and predict anything in this sport, it seems only a matter of time before some European equivalent of the NHL is established. You only need to look at other sports, football and both rugby codes, for instance, to see that there has been a trend of increased participation in European competitions for some years now. In hockey, the European Cup has been running since 1965 – though British teams have only been taking part since 1983 – but the emergence of the European Hockey League, and the coincidental, but well-timed arrival of arena hockey here, suggests to me that ultimately, the future of top level hockey in Britain may lie in international competition.

Before, British teams would have been too weak to have merited much attention in any such scheme, but the increasing successes of Sheffield, Cardiff and Manchester in recent seasons against top quality sides have done much to gain credibility for the British game in Europe. Add to this the fact that facility-wise, Britain could easily have three or four teams playing in arenas as good as anywhere on the continent, and the fact that in terms of market size, Britain has more potential than traditional hockey countries like Finland and Norway, then it increasingly looks like a franchise-based European league is going to see Britain as a key area. 'Who knows what's going to happen?' asks Shudra. 'You could have three teams left standing in Britain and they could be the three teams that are in Europe. It could be just as good a league as the internal.' It is something the Superleague seem mindful of too. The much maligned Express Cup would probably have been a more interesting competition had some continental sides, as was originally the plan, been able to take part. Where all this might lead to, I wouldn't like to say, and even if it seems unlikely that domestic hockey will ever be completely replaced by international competition – other countries would be no more keen on forfeiting their domestic competitions than we would here – it still seems likely that we will see more and more of it in the future. For hockey fanatics, it is an enticing prospect. Not only would we get the chance to see different teams and players, but we would also get to see different styles of hockey.

British ice hockey, which has always been led and dominated by Canadians, is unsurprisingly very North American in style. Originally, hockey in Canada evolved through a blend of lacrosse and rugby. The game became noted for its physical aspects, and spirit, strength and passion became the defining characteristics of the game there. In Europe, hockey evolved more from football and shinty, with a greater emphasis on teamwork and skill. Interestingly, this means that even if Britain's cultural links with Canada did not exist, it is likely that our imports would always have been North American, as European players would tend to rely more on teamwork, rather than individual skill, and a solitary Canadian would be more likely to make an impact on a British team short of talent than a solitary Swede, or Finn. Though these distinctions have become increasingly blurred as the NHL has become more global in its influence, it is still largely true to say that when a European team takes on a North American styled team, there will not only be a clash between two teams, but a clash of cultures, with the refereeing having a profound effect on the outcome.

The Steelers, and Ron Shudra, found this out for themselves when they entered the European Cup for the second time and made it to the semi-final round in Finland. In the end, they acquitted themselves well, gaining a fantastic point against the home club, Hameenlinna, and losing narrow encounters with the other two sides, but even if the results suggested that British hockey had come a long way in closing the skill gap with the top European sides, the nature of the games, particularly a bad-tempered 7–5 loss to Storhamar of Norway, suggested that there was still a massive difference in playing styles, and perhaps equally significant, in the ways in which the game was called by the officials over there.

'They don't like a very physical style,' noted Shudra. 'When we went over there we were called for a lot of roughing penalties that just were, huh, you know . . . as a player you just shake your head going: "There was nothing wrong with that hit. There was absolutely nothing wrong."' European hockey is also noted for its accepted culture of diving – imported from football, but an abhorrence to Canadians. There are few better ways to wind up a Canadian team than by employing the art. 'You touch someone with your stick and the guy takes a dive.

They call that. We found that out in Finland. The Norwegian team were . . . were *ridiculous*,' Shudra recalls. That game, which the Sheffield club led 4–1 at one stage, eventually went to the Norwegians as the referee, conditioned to a different style of hockey, had trouble adjusting to the Canadian style of play. Shudra remembers how frustrating it had been for the players to be continually called for instances which would have been tolerated and accepted in Britain. 'Finally, we just gave up and we started running them through the boards. If you're going to fall down every time we touch you with a stick, well, forget it. We're not going to touch you with a *stick* any more. If we're going to take a penalty, we're going to take a penalty – and you're going to *know* about it. And that was the way we responded. You're not going to take a penalty by hooking someone down. You're going to take a penalty by trying to put him into next week. Neither way is the right way to play the game – but one way is chicken-shit and one way isn't. Now I'll let you figure out which one's which.'

Whilst Shudra's reaction is entirely understandable, it is also clearly the voice of someone raised the Canadian way. For many, many years, Canadian hockey was universally recognised as the best in the world. From this there sprang the slightly arrogant view that if Canadian hockey was the best in the world, then everything about it must be the best. In 1972, though, things started to change. That year, for the first time, the NHL stars played a series of games against Russia, expecting to beat them eight games to nil, but, in the end, scraped through only with a winning goal in the last 34 seconds of the final game. The series had been a massive shock to Canada. The Russians had been more skilful, more organised and better conditioned than the Canadians, and it had been a wake-up call to all those who had believed that the game in North America could learn nothing from the game in Europe. Since then, the Canadian game has adapted and improved as more European players have made an impact in the NHL, but there persist certain myths about European hockey that some Canadians still cling to. For one, the idea that European players 'don't like it up 'em' – which perhaps explains why the Steelers got more physical against the Norwegians, though in that instance it doesn't seem to have proved an effective way of playing against them.

Personally, there is much about the European style of hockey I find attractive. Better skating, more skill, less brute force and more artistry. When Manchester played host to TPS Turku of Finland in the European Hockey League, in true trainspotting fashion I went along to the game early just so as to see them warm up. They were a joy to watch. For ten minutes, as they quickly ran through their drills, they just blew me away, and I saw more skill and flair in their warm-up routine than I was to see all season in the Storm's games that year (not saying a lot, mind). They not only looked different, they *sounded* different, too. When you listen to a British team on a warm up, when the crowd is yet to come in and there is no music going, you can hear the crunching sound of their skates cutting up the ice. The Turku team were all such beautifully fluid skaters that despite the pace at which they played, they made almost no sound. Like one of my school pal's noxious flatulence, which would slowly engulf an entire room with a repellent odour, they were 'silent but deadly'. They won the game with embarrassing ease, and later won the tournament itself. It didn't seem in the least bit 'chicken–shit' to me.

Shudra, though, is happy to play the style of game we are used to in Britain. 'Yeah, it's a more physical style. Which is fine. I don't mind the physical style. I would rather have guys trying to run you through the boards, than take a stick and try to break your arms,' he says, alluding to the fact that a lot more stickwork, both legal and illegal, goes on in the European game. Although the standard of hockey in Britain has improved almost beyond recognition in recent seasons, Shudra doesn't feel the actual style has altered. 'It's not changed that much, I don't think. I mean last year Newcastle tried to change, and bring in all the European guys, but they just didn't like the physical style of play. They just didn't like it, and they couldn't play. As soon as teams started to realise, well, all you have to do is finish checks, and make one hit on this guy, or hit this guy once or twice, then you don't see him the rest of the game. And that's what everybody did.'

Although he recognises that many Europeans are fine players, Shudra doesn't feel that a hockey team can survive on skill alone. 'You have to have a skilled team that has physical presence as well. You need to have a mixture of both. You need to have your skilled players, and you need to have your grinders that'll muck it out in the boards – because without them, the skilled players don't get the puck.' The grinders are also able to provide protection. 'To me, the skilled players, they're the ones you have to look after,' explains Shudra. 'They're the ones that are out there getting paid to score goals, and if some dum-dum from the other team goes after them to cause trouble, well you're going to have to take care of them. And how do you take care of them? You know, well, you get in the way of the other guy. So he's gotta come through you. And you're not going to let him come through. And that's basically when the fights start out.'

Fighting, of course, is what hockey is most famous for. Sadly. Whilst I don't deny that fights can be fun for the crowd to watch, and probably puts some bums on seats in the first place, I also suspect that it is the thing that has held the sport back the most. When you are used to watching the game, fights don't seem that important. Sure, it may be part of the reason you are drawn to the game initially, but its novelty soon wears off, and ultimately it is the rest of the game, the skill, the passion, the goals, that draw you back. Whenever hockey gets a sneering write-up, or a snide remark in the popular press, it is usually the violence aspect that is used to deride ice hockey as a whole, and articles like these are massively damaging to the sport in Britain. Don't get me wrong, I enjoy seeing Nicky Chinn punched in the face as much as the next guy, but for every fan who comes along to hockey to see a fight, how many are kept away by it? Of course, no one can really say, but there remains the lingering suspicion that fighting is off-putting to many, and we may need to ask if we really need it. Hockey is a fantastic game. Without fighting, it would still be a fantastic game.

Whilst sensitive to arguments like these, Shudra, speaking from a player's perspective, is able to tolerate it. 'Fights are part of the game. It has its time and its place. You don't want to see it every game, in every situation, but it does have its place. I think it's fine. I know all the fans here, I think they enjoy it. The guys don't go out there intentionally trying to do it, but again that's frustration creeping into the game. You know if a guy is hooking a guy all down the ice, or slashing him, and the ref doesn't call it, the next time the guy goes out and does the same, so the guy is going to get more and more frustrated. Finally he's just going to blow and he's either going to turn around and baseball the guy, or punch him in the head. Me, as a player, I'd rather get punched in the head, than whacked by a stick.'

Speaking to Shudra, you can tell that although he enjoys playing hockey in Britain, he enjoys living here too. The two don't always go hand in hand. In the time he's been here, there've been hundreds of players who, despite being able enough players, haven't been able to settle like he has. A lot of the time, Shudra feels, they simply get homesick. 'They have to be able to adapt. I mean, they're a long way from home, and it's a little bit of a culture shock coming into a different country, and different lifestyle and different people. You have to be ready for change. You have to be wanting to go out in the community and look around the town or the city. To enjoy yourself. If you're going to sit at home and do nothing, then you may as well not be here.'

Of course, plenty of Canadian players end up in Europe, where it's not so surprising that they may struggle with cultural differences. 'That's the main thing,' agrees Shudra. 'If you go to Germany, or Italy or Austria and they're speaking all their native languages – and especially if you can't speak the language – you go in there and you have no idea what's going on. You have absolutely none. There's lot of examples of guys who go to Germany but who come back the next year. They say "Oh, it was great to play there. I'd go back in a minute, but I can't understand what anyone is saying . . . " They can't get over this obstacle.' But surely, I always thought, Britain isn't so different from North America that it would cause guys problems. But, according to Shudra, if they don't make the effort, it can. 'You have to make a little bit of an effort to be in the community as well. That started in the first year with me, going out meeting and talking to everyone. That was a big thing of it, that, you know, gave me an advantage that maybe some of the guys coming later didn't have. Because the fans have had a rapport with me for eight years. The best thing you can do is not change in those eight years. Still be approachable, so everyone can come and talk to you.'

Consistency of character, feels Shudra, is important. In fact, consistency in everything is something he sets great store by. 'Consistent is the best thing anyone can be. If you're playing well, and you're consistent, then you're going to do well. If you're up and down it's no good. You can't have too many peaks and valleys. You have to be on a line. In anything, in any job you do. If you have good days and bad days at the office, or whatever, then you'd better hope that you don't have too many of the bad ones or you'll be out. You can't take things for granted.' Hockey is no different. 'You can't just turn it on when you want to. There are too many variables in the game. You can't get cocky and arrogant, you have to remember people are still coming to watch. You have to take care of them, or there won't be a team.'

There is also something particularly about Sheffield that Shudra likes. 'People here are great. They work very hard and they expect you to work hard when they come to watch you. They'll stand behind you as long as they feel you're doing the best that you can do. I enjoy the city. There's lots to do. The area, there's so much to do in the area. If you look at within 60 miles, what can you do? There's tons of stuff within an hour's drive. That gets back to going out and being in the community. Go out and sightsee within the area. If you're going to sit at home and be miserable then . . . where's the sense? You've got all that time after your training. Go out. Go for a drive. Go see the countryside. Go have lunch in a different village.' It's important for your own state of mind, argues Shudra, to try and make the best of the area you're living in. There have been players who have arrived in Britain and promptly decided that they hated it.

For Shudra, life in Britain needn't be treated any differently to how it would be back home. 'Well I always liked to do things. I'm that kind of person. Back in the States, or Canada I still wanted to go out. In Halifax I'd still go out in the area and see what I could see. I wouldn't just sit in the house.' At this point, we both got distracted by the fact he'd played in one Halifax back home, and was now playing so close to the original in Yorkshire. 'Oh yeah. No kidding. I'd never thought of that. Yeah, it's right there. I've never been! That's one place I haven't been. I'll have to do that. You have to go and experience the atmosphere of these places . . .'

If not every player is going to be smart enough to make the most from their spell playing here, Shudra thinks that at least they'll enjoy the hockey more now. The Superleague has brought about a level of competition and professionalism that is increasingly getting noticed on the hockey grapevine. 'Guys will know from other guys,' says Shudra, when I ask him how aware of British hockey players in North America are. 'Whenever you go back in the summer you always know a lot of other players. And they ask, "How was it?" and you'll say, "Oh, it was great. You should see it. The league was as good as the American Hockey League" or whatever it was, and players will go, "Oh, jeese. It sounds pretty good over there." As long as the money is okay, or it's the same as what they're going to get back home. Back home they play 100 games, and here for the same money you play 50. As long as it's the same calibre, what would you choose? It's a chance to see something different.'

You get the impression that Shudra, who has been one of the guys who's done the most to help British hockey get where it is, is pretty pleased by the way things have gone here. Does he feel proud of British hockey? 'I think so, yeah. It's gone leaps and bounds in the last few years. There's a lot of good British guys around that weren't around before. You look in our league, or in the league below, which pretty much is all British, and there're some pretty good players there.' In the years he's been here, Shudra has noticed a few changes in the level of British players. 'They're more skilful. They think quicker. They're faster on their feet. They work a little harder.' But at the same time, Shudra appreciates that under the current system, a lot of good talent is going to waste as once players emerge from junior hockey their opportunities become limited. 'If they have a goal, and they know that people are watching them, then they'll go out and work very hard to try and get that goal. But they have to have the place to play after they've done their under 15, 16, 18 or whatever. They have to have somewhere to go afterwards. If they don't, then they don't care, and it becomes more of a hobby.'

You get the impression when you talk to Ron Shudra, that he is a very level-headed bloke. He's intelligent, rational and pragmatic. A friendlier, more approachable guy you couldn't wish to meet. For my needs, this is clearly a nightmare. Obviously, I can't have anyone in this book coming across as more intelligent than I am. (I'm not insecure – and I'll deck anyone who says I am.) So in order to make him suddenly look foolish, I had to bring out the big guns and ask him about superstitions. Hockey is probably the most superstitious sport I've ever come across. Come play-off time, your favourite team will all start to wear improbable, and often laughable beards because of the North American tradition of not shaving in the play-offs until you get knocked out. This folly persists here even though our play-off format is different, and the team that wins the play-offs here will only have had to play an extra week or so longer than anyone else, rather than the six or seven weeks it might be across the pond.

And it's not just the players; it can be the fans too. Famously, in Detroit they used to throw octopuses on the ice whenever the Red Wings scored a play-off goal. The idea was that in the golden age of the game, the 'Original Six' era, you had to win eight games to win the Stanley Cup and the eight tentacles of the octopus represented each of those games. This superstition persisted even into the modern game, despite the fact that by now you had to win 16 games to capture the prize. It was only last season that the whole nonsense was stopped when league officials claimed it was taking too long to clear the ice after the Red Wings scored, and banned fans from hurling dead molluscs over the plexi-glass. Needless to say, once the superstition was abandoned, the Red Wings promptly won their first Stanley Cup for 42 years.

But superstitions are not just a play-off phenomenon. Every player I've ever spoken to admits to always dressing a certain way, and maybe always sitting on the same seat in the team bus, and maybe always being the second last player to leave the ice after a game and maybe always being the last guy to shoot the puck at the goalie during the warm up, and maybe always driving to the arena the same way, and maybe half a dozen other crazy things that they've been far too smart to actually tell anyone about. Like many players, Shudra is far too smart to believe in them, yet not so stupid as to defy them. Immediately, and for the first time in our interview, his tone became somewhat more bashful once I raised the subject. I put it to him that hockey was the most superstitious sport I had ever come across.

'I don't know what it is, to be honest, but it is. You see it right from goalies all the way out. Guys always putting their left skate on first, then their right elbow pads. Or they don't put their skates on 'til they've got all their equipment on, or they put their skates on first . . . I've put tape on the same way for the last ten years I think. Ever since I started playing pro, I've not changed *anything*. I start on the left side. I do my left side then my right side. All the way up my body. From putting my left sock on first, to putting my right arm through my shirt last. It's not so much a superstition, it's become habit now.' Yeah, but if it's just a habit then why not break it? 'I wouldn't. I couldn't,' he says, laughing but serious. 'Is that superstition or habit? It feels good to have it like that, and to change it, uh, I'd have to try it in practice first. I couldn't do something that drastic like tape my stick differently in a game!' You consider taping your stick differently as 'drastic'? 'Oh yeah. That's drastic,' he admits.

I felt kind of bad about teasing him like this, because although superstitions are silly, fatuous nonsense, I can understand why players have them. Games are so uncontrollable, so unpredictable, that it is understandable for a player to want to ritualise as many things connected with the game as possible, to restore some semblance of order amongst all the things they have no control over. There is also the fact that always getting dressed a certain way, or tapping the goalie's pads with your stick before the game commences, and always taping your stick the same way – even if the tape doesn't need to be changed – can be part of your mental preparation. To go through the same things in exactly the same sequence before every game in order to get your mind set. 'It's what you do to get prepared before a game,' Shudra suggests. This mental preparation needn't always involve superstitions, though. 'Everybody does something a little different. Whether it be listening to a Walkman, or just sitting, having a coffee and reading the programme, or just being dressed ready for the game 20 minutes before it starts. Everybody does their own thing.' But it's definitely the superstitions that are the interesting ones.

I know a player who always used to put his left boot on before his right. For years he did this, and never ever thought about changing it. Then one day, moments before a game, there was some problem, either a lace snapped, or the blade needed to be sharpened, and there was so little time to go before face-off that he had no choice but to put his right boot on first whilst an assistant sorted out the left. In the nick of time, he quickly put his left boot on, but felt uneasy that the hockey gods might be angered by this treachery. He skated out, acutely unsettled, but immediately scored a couple of goals, and then had his best game for several months. You would think that the incident would have shown him that the whole thing had obviously been irrelevant. All those years of doing something a certain way because he was afraid he'd have a bad game if he didn't obey a certain routine. This enforced departure obviously hadn't brought him bad luck, so what did it matter? He agreed with me wholeheartedly as I put this to him, and admitted that as a result, he had abandoned this silly idea of always putting his right boot on last. Now, he always puts his *left* boot on last.

'I'm not quite that bad, but I know there's been guys that don't wash their underwear for two weeks in the play-offs,' confesses Shudra. 'It's crazy. You're begging them to do something about it and they won't . . . We're over the top sometimes.' Apart from providing psychologists with incriminating evidence of disturbed psyches, superstitions can also have an up-side, feels Shudra. 'They're actually a lot of fun sometimes; superstitions. They can be. Especially when you sit beside someone for so long, or you're sitting across from someone and you actually sit back and watch them. You nudge the guy sat next to you and you say, "Look at this. Watch this. Watch the way he does this." You ask the guy why he does it, and you kind of take the piss out of each other for it. It adds to the camaraderie. You can have a good group, and be very close. Take the piss and have a lot of fun doing it. Nothing malicious about it. And superstition is one of those things that brings that out.'

I like talking to players about superstitions. Sometimes when you interview players, and talk about certain aspects of the game, you get the feeling they aren't really talking with their own words at all. They rely on stock phrases to get them through the interview, and although many of them are very bright, they are rarely able, or perhaps inclined, to shed any new light on a subject. But ask a guy to talk about taping his stick. Sure, he'll look at you kind of funny, but when he knows you're serious, he'll tell you in intricate detail how he does it. About the pleasure he gets from doing it. The reassurance it gives him. The same satisfaction a carpenter gets from looking after his tools properly. And then you realise it is the real player talking to you, opening up, showing you how much hockey is part of him, and how much he loves it. And then, obviously, you're compelled to take the piss out of him . . .

So in a sport where so many players come and go, Ron Shudra stands out as someone who came to Britain determined to do the best job he could. The fact that he's still here is testament to how successful he's been. It hasn't turned out the way he envisioned it. 'It's always been a seat of the pants thing,' he admits. 'You can never predict success, you just hope you don't fail.' And typically, he's modest about the role he's had in establishing the Steelers, and the influence he has had on the British game. 'Well, every year there's been a challenge. I've been lucky to stay here. The fans like me here, I'm happy here, so if I can stay here I will.' And unless 'something drastic happens' he sees the rest of his playing career being spent in Britain.

But his has been a strange journey, even for a hockey player. His pro career started out with glimpses of the top, he dropped down a level, then jumped across the sea to find an ocean of difference. Starting at the top. Sliding a hell of a long way down, but then climbing back up in style. Ironically, though he's taken a hell of a detour, the standard of hockey he's playing now is not too far from the leagues he started off in. 'It's very close to where it was when I started,' he concedes, as though it's the first time the thought has struck him. 'So you've gone full circle, then?' I suggested, hoping to prompt him into an insightful soundbite I could finish on. 'Well, that's good then,' he said, simply, which made me laugh, for some reason. It would be fair to say Ron's a no-nonsense kind of guy.

Perhaps to the surprise of the kid who once sat in a locker-room full of stars, he has become one himself on another continent – though, as he'll admit, Britain is still a long way from the NHL. He's got no regrets, though. 'I've had a great time doing it. I've experienced a lot of things, and if I had a chance to do things again, I would do it again in a second. All the way. I made the right choice when I was younger, let's put it that way. I think I did.' And of course, he's not finished yet. Now 30, he's still got a lot of hockey left in him, but because he always seemed like a veteran – even when he was a kid – being one now sits comfortably with him. He knows, as all players do, that it will come to an end all too soon though. Like everything else, Shudra is realistic about it. 'When I'm ready to hang up the boots I'll hang them up,' he says, with no obvious sound of regret. 'And when will that be?' I asked him. 'Ooh, hopefully not for about another 25 more years . . . '

Top man.

THIRD PERIOD

The Head Honcho

It's funny. When they win they get more of the credit than they really should, and when they lose they get more of the blame than they deserve. Every club needs one, yet no kid ever set out on his hockey career wanting to be one. They get little adulation, though plenty of abuse. It is the most demanding, complex and arduous job in the sport, and one that demands many more different skills than you would normally expect to find in any single individual. Yet every fan I've met has their own opinions on how it could, and should, be done better at their own club. They surround themselves with hand-picked colleagues who they hope they can depend upon, yet in the final analysis, they have the loneliest job in ice hockey. Welcome to the world of the head coach.

Born on the last day of 1960, Manchester Storm's Kurt Kleinendorst was hockey mad from day one. A skilled forward, he represented the USA in the World Championships and made it to the Winter Olympics in 1984. After several years playing in North America and Europe, he started to dabble in coaching when he was made the player-coach of ERC Selb, in Germany – whilst still only 27 years old. After surviving this trauma intact, he later returned to America and got his first head coach job in Raleigh, when the ECHL's Ice Caps were formed in 1991. The transition from player to coach, however, was not without its problems. For one thing, there was a certain amount of culture shock. I asked him how hard it had been.

'You know what? It's very eye-opening. I recall going through my first job interview, and I'll tell you, you say all the right things, you know what you need to say, you know you've got to convince whoever it is that's going to hire you that they'd be foolish not to hire you. And then you get the job and it's like "Oh my gosh." You know, "What have I done? Am I ready for this?" Because as a player you have *absolutely no clue* as to the detail or the depth of what it takes to be a coach.' Part of the problem, explains Kurt, is that as a player you are necessarily self-centred. 'You don't really have to deal with the psyches of your teammates. You worry about yourself. As a player you don't really have to sit there and analyse and evaluate how defencemen play different situations when you are a forward. And when you are a centre you don't really think about the left winger's responsibility, or the right winger. You just have to worry about yourself. As a coach you have to worry about *everything*. You have to worry about your practice plans. You have to worry about what you want to accomplish on a Monday, on a Tuesday, on a Wednesday, on a Thursday – when you've got a game on a Saturday. You need to know how long your practices need to be. And you need to know what your opponent is going to be like. You need to work on your systems, and you need to think about your players' psyches, and on and on and on . . .'

Considering how different the two jobs are, then, I wondered if being a player beforehand was a necessary qualification for the job of coach. That, although everyone would expect it to be the perfect training, it does in fact lead you into the position so ill-prepared that you'd have been better going into the job from a fresh perspective where you don't have any preconceived notions about it. 'If you've been a student of the game, sure, you could be a coach,' concedes Kleinendorst, 'but I don't know many coaches in this particular sport that haven't been players. It's a great background.' For one thing, there is the fact that players are more likely to respect what a coach is saying when they know he has played the game himself, but more than that, argues Kleinendorst, having been a player does give you an insight into details that may not be apparent to someone who has never actually played the game.

'From a coaching standpoint, hockey can be very in-depth,' he explains, 'and there's a lot of teaching points and techniques that can be taught to help your guys be better – I'm a teaching coach, I probably teach more than most. But if you've not played, I don't know where you can get the experience to teach those things. You could read about it, sure, but still, reading and experiencing are two different things. There are things that, I don't want to say are difficult, but which are complicated if you don't have a hockey background. I mean, for example, breakouts. Hockey is a game where you have to react to situations – I don't know that any two are identical, although there are very many that are similar. But, just for example, when it comes to breakouts, depending on what the situation is, there are anywhere from eight to ten different breakouts. Now if you're not a hockey person, I'm sure you could figure it out, but it might not come real easy . . . '

Of course, there have been coaches, who despite being ex-players themselves, have been successful without necessarily having a great grasp of the technical nuances of the game. In Britain, particularly a few years ago, coaches with very little technical appreciation could always get by providing they had a good eye for talent, or were good motivators. As Dave Biggar recalls from his early days with Sheffield, these motivational techniques weren't always particularly elegant or sophisticated – 'I remember standing at the side of the Steelers bench – Ronnie Wood was in charge at the time, and he was after one of the players on the other team because he was hurting the Steelers, and Ronnie was sellotaping £20 notes to the plexiglass. And I said, "What on earth are you doing?" and he said, "Oh, it's just an incentive. Whoever decks [whatever the name of the guy was] pulls a £20 note off. Whoever gets him out of the game gets £100."'

Strange though this sort of thing might sound today, there was plenty of this going on in the British game at the time. Then, in the days of teams just having two or three import players, coaching was more a matter of simply knowing when to open the gate to put your best players on the ice. In the 1993/94 season, for instance, the Trafford Metros' three top imports accounted for 77 per cent of their team's goals at an average of over 100 goals each. The top goal-scoring Brit on the team, Paul Broadhurst – who played more games than any of them that season – scored, erm, 12 goals. Hockey in Britain at this time was fairly rudimentary, and it was generally assumed that imports would know more about the game than their British coaches anyway, so the coaches would just let the imports get on with it, and concentrate on motivating their teams.

Of course, this was not always that difficult. Generally, teams would consist mainly of local lads, and the argument was that they would often play their hearts out for their team because they genuinely cared about it. When local pride was at stake, it was simple for coaches to get the troops fired up. However, as more imports arrived into the game, things became a little more difficult for coaches. These new arrivals, whilst they might be better players in almost every respect, tended to be a little more mercenary about things, and so perhaps more difficult to motivate. They were there to earn a living, rather than to fight to prove forever that Whitley was better than Billingham, for instance.

They also expected to be coached more. Previously, in a penalty killing situation, for instance, a coach would just open the gate and let his imports deal with things. Now, with teams having rosters full of imports, you couldn't just expect your key players to dominate so easily. Now, in order to get the edge, you didn't just tell them when to play, but *how* to play. Did they play a box shape defence? A diamond formation? In truth, not every coach was particularly clued up on this sort of thing. To them, a left wing lock would simply be something you found on Ken Livingston's head. The Superleague brought this failing of the old school of coaching into sharper focus as increasingly coaches found that their new players demanded more of the kind of coaching they had been used to back home. Having said that, it was still possible for teams to be successful, even if their coach wasn't exactly Scotty Bowman.

When John Lawless left Cardiff to start the Manchester Storm, Paul Heavey was moved, reluctantly at first, into his head coach job. Smart enough to realise that there were guys in his team who might be able to help him adapt to the job, he openly called on their help. Randy Smith, one of Heavey's first signings, thought that this honesty was one of the reasons the team was successful. 'We had guys who grew up with hockey,' he recalls. 'That's nothing against the British guys, but it would be like me coming over here after playing soccer in Canada when I was ten or eleven, and then saying, "Okay, now I'm coaching Newcastle United." That would be impossible. So when Paul Heavey took over as coach, he grew up in Britain playing hockey, and probably never really had any real coaching himself. I mean, you've got guys now who've been coached by guys in the NHL, or Olympics teams, and who know hockey, so we helped Paul out. He did an outstanding job. I think the best thing about him was that he said "Look, I'm going to try and be the coach, but I don't know everything. So if you see I'm doing something wrong, help me, or just say." Whereas I think a lot of guys get into trouble because they say, "Oh, I'm the coach now. All of a sudden, I know everything."'

Heavey, though, was different. 'I think he knew that he didn't know enough about it,' feels Smith. 'I think he's a real hard worker, and he wants to know things before he gets involved. He read a lot of books, he watched a lot of videos, he went to coaching seminars, and he tried to learn, whereas a lot of guys would have just said, "Hey, I don't need to do any of that because I've played hockey for 20 years and now I'm a coach and I know." I think that's part of the reason guys wanted to play for him. If he had just come in and pretended to be this hard-ass, you know, "It's my way or the highway," I think guys might have rebelled. He laid it on the line, but would say, "I don't know for sure, so help me out here." And the guys rallied round him, because we saw he really cared, and he wanted to win worse than anyone. And they played for him, and it paid off.' In the first year of the Superleague, Heavey, the most inexperienced coach in the league, led the Devils to the title.

Increasingly though, this kind of player-led coaching would be the exception, though even in the second year of the Superleague there were one or two teams who got by on it. 'I'm not going to be specific, but there's a team in our league right now that, basically, the players are just coaching themselves,' says Kleinendorst. 'You know, where the coach is a motivator, and he motivates them by fear, but when all is said and done, the players are the ones who are actually, you know, thinking things through for their team. And I know this because of things that have been said to my players, and something that has been said to me specifically. And so, from my end, that's just very interesting. But that shows you how much motivation plays into winning. Right there. Because the team I'm talking about is having a very successful season. And it just goes to show you that if you can get your guys motivated, and prepared to play, you can be successful. I really believe that one of the things that leads to success within a team, is that you have to be a group that gets along and you *have* to be a group that is committed to working hard. And if you work hard, you are going to win most nights. You really will. So now, if you've got a group of guys that play together as a team, and they work hard every night, and they are on the same page, within a system – to me that's pretty unbeatable. But the frustrating part for a coach is to get that to happen.'

The key to this sort of thing is discipline. If a coach has a disciplined side then not only are they more likely to try and play within a gameplan, but they are also less likely to get thown off it by intimidation. Often, you will see a team try and rough up the opposition to try and throw them off their gameplan, but this isn't the only way you can try and unsettle an opponent. Anyone who has sat close enough to the playing surface to hear what players sometimes say to each other will testify that dirty tricks don't always involve sticks. 'You wouldn't believe some of the things they say about your mother,' reveals Kurt. 'After a while, you just learn. I think the key to discipline, and playing a disciplined game, is simple. You initiate – you don't retaliate. You get your nose in there, you make the hit, you know, and then if they do something stupid you don't retaliate because that's usually the guy that gets it. So when you go in and you make a nice play, they do something stupid – there's your retaliation, there's your two-minute minor, whatever it is, and then you get on the powerplay. You want to get in their faces, play an aggressive game, but you don't want to be taking yourself off your own game. We get whacked, and hacked and smacked, but we don't lose our focus. It's not easy, 'cos some of those things sting a little bit.' Not that Kurt's team are always saints, themselves. Sometimes, carrying an unpleasant persona can help the team. You don't want to be too nice out there. 'You know what? Nasty is good,' Kurt told me after one game, when, unusually, the Storm had been forced to play a more physical style. 'When you can dislike who you're playing against a little bit it actually helps the level of your game. Within the rules. Not so nasty that it takes it away from the other parts of the game. You know, I mean, there's a fine line between being a little bit of a prick and going overboard where you're not in control of your emotions. You have to be in control of your emotions.' More than ever, this is important. Before, teams could lose their tempers for a spell, then still get it together and turn things around to win the game. Now, though, the team that played a disciplined game for the full 60 minutes was likely to come out on top.

A natural consequence of the improved standard of hockey in Britain has been a dramatic fall in the number of goals scored. In their debut season, playing in the old British League Division One, the Manchester Storm rattled in an average of 10.36 goals per game. The very next season, playing in the inaugural Superleague with an improved squad, that figure dropped to 3.38. Suddenly, winning margins were not five or six goals every game, but now only one or two goals (and for the Storm winning margins were now usually called 'losing margins'). Whereas, in the old Premier League, you could safely predict the outcome of almost every match, now, in the Superleague, things were getting too close to call. 'Nothing is taken for granted,' says Panthers coach Mike Blaisdell. 'It used to be, you could look at your schedule and see seven wins, and then say, "Oh, but those next two after that will be tough." But no more. It's every game now.' With games now being so close, it increasingly came down to the little things that decided whether or not games were won. That put an increasing strain on the coaches who found that the margin for error was decreasing all the time.

'When you are trying to motivate 20 guys in a team sport, where every guy plays a part on every night, and the difference between winning and losing can only be a matter of one play, it really ties your hands tremendously,' admitted Kurt to me the night after the Storm had gone down by a single late goal in Nottingham. 'Last night would be a perfect example. We played a very good game, but we had certain individuals in last night's game who were not prepared for a shift – like *one* shift. One situation *within* that shift. Not prepared mentally, and then physically, to carry it out. But, my point is, being unprepared for that one moment cost us the game. And it only has to be one situation. But that's hockey. That's the thing about the mental part of this game. This game is a physical game, guys have to know how to skate, shoot, all that other stuff, you know, the physical parts of it, but when all is said and done it's the group of guys who are the strongest mentally, and are most committed, who are going to get it done.'

So, having said that, when in the modern game it is increasingly important that a coach prepares his players thoroughly, how does a coach motivate his players? I asked Kurt if a coach had to be smart to get the best from his squad. 'It depends. "Smart" how? In what way?' he asked, smartly. '*Smart* is finding a way to make your team win. You have to be smart enough, and intelligent enough, to figure out what it's going to take for your guys to win.' Of course, that isn't to say that a great motivator need be a great intellect. Sometimes, a guy might not be the brightest bloke in the world but something about him makes players want to do their best for him. Rocky Saganiuk, for instance, despite not being blessed with the most talented British teams ever assembled, managed to bully, coax and inspire his teams to far greater performances than he had any right to. In Canada, Don Cherry (who certainly *isn't* the brightest guy in the world) had an amazing track record as a coach by employing all sorts of dubious tricks. Kleinendorst recalls one famous story:

'There's a story about Don Cherry where he had a curfew, but at the same time he had called a meeting to get the players down to the bar. And they were down in the bar, and he came walking in, looked around, and just walked right out with a real mad look on his face. Then he let it be filtered through his team that "Had they forgotten about the curfew?" That they sure as shit better come out the next night and win – it was in LA, I think, or else there would be hell to pay. Well, they just came out and *smoked* them because they were scared to death of him. So that's Don Cherry. That's the way he worked. Motivator. He was really smart at finding ways to get his players to play. He was one of those coaches that used psychology.' By his own admission, it's not a tactic that Kleinendorst would use.

'I'm not a head-game coach. I don't mess with my guys' heads. I challenge them outright – to come out and play intelligent. To come out and play hard and let's have a good night. But Don Cherry would play head-games. He would do things to make his players think things, that would get them to play. Now, I would *never* do something like that.' The tactics of fear, of course, are ones that are widely used in North America. All it takes for a player to have his career shattered is for one coach to take a dislike to him, and to then let word filter around the leagues that that player has an attitude problem, and then the player may suddenly find that no other team wants to hire him. (It's not unknown for victims of this to be forced to look to Europe, where the hockey grapevine is not so vindictive, in an effort to find work.) In this country, players usually don't find it so hard to find another team to play for, as there is less competition amongst players for places, but that's not to say that the tactics of fear aren't employed here too. As dressing room doors and broken cutlery across many rinks will testify, coaches here have been known to get a little upset with their players.

As a coach, blowing your top with your players can often be a devastating tactical card to play. Players who have got themselves in a complacent rut, or who perhaps feel the coach lacks authority or conviction, and can be taken advantage of, are often given a nasty shock when that coach then turns around and goes ballistic in front of them. It can often clear the air, force players to look honestly at their own performance or inspire teams to greater efforts, but it can also be a dangerous card to play. Apart from being bad news for a coach's blood pressure, it can also backfire and cause resentment if players don't feel it is justified. It's also true to say that the more often the ballistic card is played, the less its impact is felt. On the whole, Kleinendorst has never been a fan of the tactic.

'It's a last resort. In fact, I try to stay away from team meetings as much as I possibly can. I don't even like to talk to my guys other than on mild little things after a game. If we lose a game, unless it's a certain situation, or it's a certain game where something really went wrong, I don't like to go in to address the guys when my emotions are wrought. I like to leave it alone and not say much at all. Then the following day, after I've thought about it a little bit and I've had a chance to watch the video, to see how good, or how bad it *really* was, I will go in and blast them. And I've found that that works pretty well for me.'

To a large extent, a coach's personality will determine the techniques open to him and shape the way he carries out his job. Kleinendorst the coach, and Kleinendorst the man are not so different. 'I'm positive. I try not to be negative. And I think that my guys realise that if I do start yelling a little bit then it's for a good reason. I try to stay positive. I think of Bob Johnson (the popular late coach of the Pittsburgh Penguins, famous for his catchphrase of "It's a great day for hockey") he was just Mr Positive. And that's more my personality, really. I'm very uncomfortable with being negative. I'm very uncomfortable with being critical. I much prefer to bring a guy in and just kind of show him, in the right tone of voice, the situation, what he did, how he should have handled it differently, as opposed to getting in someone's face and being critical. My philosophy is treat guys the way you'd like to be treated. Even as a player, I would much prefer for the coach to bring me in and just say, "Hey, listen. You know you could do better than what you're doing" – in the right way. Rather than give it to me in front of the group of guys. That's embarrassing.'

Not every coach is as nice to his players as Kleinendorst. The very mention of the name Mike Keenan in US hockey circles is often enough to strike fear into players' hearts. Famed for a 'win at all costs' mental toughness, Keenan has been known to reduce players to sobbing wrecks under some of his humiliating coaching methods. 'But guys like playing for him,' says Kurt. 'Because they play on the edge, with fear. But most times they'll be successful. Guys really want to be successful I think, when all is said and done. I mean, they'll play for Moses, if Moses can help them win. That's really what the guys want. They want a coach who can lead them to winning. You were here last year, you saw what it was like,' he says, referring to the year when the Storm went from winning 94 per cent of their games the previous season to a dispiriting 33 per cent in the first Superleague season under John Lawless, who was later sacked as a result. 'A lot of guys, with everything that they've got here, wouldn't have been back this year because they didn't want to go through another year like last year. Guys just want to win. It's not good if you can't win. If you can't be at least .500, you're miserable. You know, if you slide under .500, where you're not winning at least every other game, it's ugly. You don't want to come to the rink.'

This was a feeling depressingly familiar to Basingstoke coach Peter Woods when I spoke to him after a game at Manchester which the Bisons had lost 5–1, their fourth defeat on the trot. 'When you start losing, sometimes it becomes a habit. Anytime you start winning I think everything's upbeat. You know, "You got a great coach, and great fans, and great players." And all of a sudden you start losing, and it's the opposite – "Your coach sucks, the fans aren't any good and the players aren't very good either." But, uhm, that's reality, that's just the way it is.' So bearing in mind how everything gets coloured by whether or not the team is winning, the pressure for a coach to keep driving his players on is immense. Clearly, he has to keep telling them what to do. But are they listening?

Anyone who has spoken to hockey players, or players of any team sport for that matter, will have noticed that they tend to speak in clichés. They'll try to stay focused and take it one game at a time. They'll give it 110 per cent. They know they just have to do the simple things and keep working hard. As long as the team wins they don't mind if they, themselves, don't score. It is all solid stuff, of course. You can't really argue with any of it. But it all sounds so familiar, so automatic, that to my cynical ears it always sounds as if they are just on auto-pilot. Just saying the things they know they are expected to say. I swear, the press conferences get more and more like *The Stepford Wives* every season. It gets boring for us to hear this stuff over and over again, but how boring must it be for the players themselves to hear it all the time? As a coach, how do you keep telling your players the same shit every game and expect them to pay any attention at all?

'Well, see, that's the thing. I mean, right now, (mid season) it's a difficult time. Early in the season it's very easy. The guys are fresh, they're receptive, they want to impress. Not just the coach, but their teammates. They want to get off to a good start. But as the season unfolds, you know, little by little, they lose the focus and the way they were at the beginning. And that's one of the hardest things, from a coaching perspective, to maintain – that mental sharpness. That's why you go through the season and you don't throw everything at your players in September, or August. You always hold little things back that you are going to throw at them next month, or whatever.'

Nevertheless, Kleinendorst will still tend to find himself re-stating the basics to his players over and over – and watching their eyes glaze over as he's doing it. 'After a while, I mean, they just let it go in here, you know, in one ear and right out the other ear. They just turn it off. And so really, I continue to go at it, but at not quite the same degree I would have earlier, because I understand. They don't need to hear it again – they don't *want* to hear it again. They don't need to hear it from me, they need to hear it from their captain. They don't need to hear it from me, they need to hear it from the guy they are stood next to in the locker room. And that's where, when you've got a good group of guys, and you have good leadership, you know, you can benefit. Because it's a matter of us being together, you know, like a system together. Doing things consistently, being predictable, for each other. You have to be. And when you get certain guys who go outside the scope of our system, and they start winging it, then you've got a different kind of situation. So I still say the same things, but not quite as much as I did before, and then I rely on my captains to get the message across.'

It has been said that coaching is analogous to parenthood. You try to raise your players the best you can, to instil in them the right set of values and the way to behave, but then once they step on the ice it's as if they have left home and are fending for themselves in a harsh environment. Kurt, playing the role of the responsible parent, feels it is his responsibility to ensure that his players are as well prepared as possible. 'You can't let them go out and just do it on their own,' he feels. 'You've got a system – though you don't want robots. I believe, in certain situations, you have to be predictable to each other in what you're doing. And then there're other instances where you can allow them to be a little more creative and freewheeling. Defensively, I think it's cut and dried. Every situation has an exact defence. You know, like *exact*. But when you go on the offensive part of the game it can change a little bit, and that's where you allow them a little more freedom in most situations, though still you're specific in others. I'll give you an example. You know if you're going down on a 3-on-2, three forwards against the other team's two defencemen, well, if you get the middle guy to drive through the net every time, and that third guy to come up late, you're going to get a quality shot on every single 3-on-2 rush that you have. So that would be one situation where, offensively, I would say, every time, "I want my middle guy driving the net." Whereas there are other times where you just have to allow them to be themselves. You have got to give them a little bit of freedom. And then in the defensive end, you don't give them freedom *at all*. They've got to be predictable. They can't start winging it, because when you start winging it in your own end you've got chaos.'

This is a problem area for coaches. Offensive talent is great to have. A lot of the time players are just born with it, and all a coach has to do in order to get the best out of his offensive talent is to simply say, 'Go out there and enjoy yourself.' Defensive play, however, is more a matter of application. When you tell your defensive players how you want them to play you are unlikely to be insisting that they have fun. 'Defensive zone play is probably the most difficult part of the game to really teach, because that's where you've got the least amount of commitment from players,' observes Kleinendorst. 'Everyone wants to play offence. Most guys don't want to make the commitment to play defensively, but if you can be good defensively, you can be very good as a team.'

This reluctance players have towards defence is easy to understand. Many players will tell you that when they were growing up as kids they would pretend that they were scoring the winning goal in the seventh game of the Stanley Cup Finals. There are very few who have ever suggested to me that they fantasised about playing a good penalty-killing shift. Sometimes, in North America, teams will employ assistant coaches who concentrate exclusively on defence. 'What you have mostly back in the NHL is an assistant who was a defenceman, who specialises in that particular field, who works with those defencemen,' explains Kleinendorst. 'The assistant is the one responsible for that defensive system. You know, the forwards and the defencemen working together in the defensive zone.' In Britain, it is less common for teams to employ someone in this way, but as the style of coaching here becomes more professional, it is perhaps something we are likely to see more of.

Whilst coaches here struggle to keep their players' minds on the task at hand, they can gain some degree of satisfaction from the fact that the media in this country, and particularly the press, tend to be less openly critical of their coaching methods than the press in North America. Partly, this is because with hockey still a developing sport, and not nearly so entrenched in our national conscience as, say, football or rugby, the role of the press is seen more as a supportive one. It is hard to envisage a newspaper campaign to oust a particular coach, or an editorial to lambast a team's playing strategy. Although individual sports reporters may be critical of a team in private, they are rarely as critical in print, because first and foremost, they want to promote the game. Even the specialised hockey press, who don't need to be as sensitive about the way they portray hockey to a readership that is already committed to the sport, tend to shy away from openly slagging off coaches. Compared to the way failure is tolerated by the press in football or cricket, it is a luxurious position for coaches in Britain to be in – a point that Kleinendorst accepts.

'You're right. I mean, if that weren't the case, I think our little stretch leading up to Christmas (when the Storm lost four games on the trot, after starting the season with just one regular time defeat in 24 games) would have been a case in point. And I know that were it not for a supportive press, there could be a lot more pressure on myself, and on my players, which I don't think would really help us at all.' So how differently would the same position have been dealt with by the press back home? 'It depends on which city you are in. If you are talking about Toronto, I mean Toronto, right now, the players and coaching staff, under the circumstances that we've got, would probably be under a tremendous amount of pressure, because they are not living up to the expectations that they created earlier in the season. So, um, I don't read a lot of the press, I just don't want to take the chance of being stung.' Which, it must be said, is a lot easier to do in Manchester than it is in Montreal, where the hockey team is placed constantly under the microscope by an expectant media.

However, in North America the attention of the press doesn't mean that there are no benefits to coaches. The competition for stories among the press corps is so fierce that it does mean that coaches can play the media to their advantage – a tactic that is rarely used on these shores. Certain coaches in the States may utilise the press to undermine players who, for example, they feel are demanding too much money, or perhaps get a critical story of a certain player run who they feel needs to be taken down a peg or two because he has been critical of the coach, or perhaps just needs something to motivate him. Such Machiavellian ploys, though, are very rare in the British game. 'I don't think I could do that,' muses Kleinendorst, 'because our press is just too complimentary. And I'm not a negative kind of guy anyway . . . ' So does this mean, if you can't manipulate the press to help you motivate your team, or whatever, then they are really more of a nuisance?

'I get along very well,' insists Kleinendorst, smiling. 'Like stuff like this, I don't mind doing this, at all. I've got absolutely no problem with the press. In fact, I'll go out of my way to help out. On short notice say. Say someone needs to do an interview – I'll do an interview. It's not that big a deal for me. I don't look at you guys as a nuisance at all. I think it's a means, you know, for us to get it out there. Because I think British ice hockey is growing, and it's growing for a lot of reasons, and the media would be one of them.' However, in the 1997/98 season there were a few signs that the media could perhaps be a bit more of a nuisance in the future. The *News of the World* which had started to devote a small column to hockey every Sunday, started to run sensationalist stories that would usually suggest some dramatic goings on within the sport. Whilst these usually made good copy, and were often entertaining, they tended to be somewhat fanciful, and in a couple of instances, caused a certain amount of distress and irritation as suggestions were made that were palpably untrue. Kurt, himself a victim on one occasion, was able to shrug them off easily enough, but as hockey gets more coverage in the future, it is likely to get more bad coverage too.

However, unlike in football, one of the things that still affects the relationship between the media and players and coaches in hockey, is the fact that a lot of the press in this country are relatively new to the sport, and they tend to be mindful of the fact that they have only a few years of watching hockey under their belts when they start to quiz people who have been immersed in the game all their lives. By contrast, every football writer I have ever met is an 'expert'. They have followed the game since they were children, and very few of them ever seem to get the feeling that they may be talking to someone who knows more about the game than they do. Hockey writers, on the other hand, tend not to be so self assured. There are many who are very knowledgeable about the game, but I don't know many who have ever actually played it for instance, and they tend to be more deferential towards coaches and players as a result. Personally, hockey interviews are rarely a chance for me to spout my own theories, like they would be if I was interviewing a football manager – I remember once having the temerity to suggest to Alex Ferguson how Roy Keane could be better used for United, which I cringe at now – but instead I see them as an opportunity to learn something new about the game. With this in mind, when speaking to Kurt, I thought I'd take the opportunity to try and learn something myself about an aspect of the game that had always puzzled me. Why was it, even after all these years of watching the game, that I was so bad at sussing out how good individual players actually were?

Often, when you have been watching a game from the press box, you are invited to vote for the man of the match. Sometimes this is easy. If a particular player has scored all five goals and reduced the opposition to shreds then it isn't going to take a genius to recognise that he has made an impact on the game. If a guy has displayed outrageous ability and thrown moves on the netminder that I have never seen before, then again, I'll tend to notice him. Likewise, it's easy, even for the novice spectator, to work out how well the netminder may have played because his job is so simply defined, and just looking at the scoreboard will give you a reasonable indication of how well he has played. (There was a spectacular exception to this at one game in Manchester when the Storm netminder, Jim Hrivnak, doing a fair impression of an alien hyperbeing from the planet Shut-out, put on the most awesome display of netminding I've ever seen, leading the Storm to a league record 47 shot shut-out of the Bracknell Bees in a 5–0 win. At the end he received a standing ovation from both sets of supporters. The man of the match award, chosen by a member of the supporters club, on this occasion, inexplicably went to a defenceman who hadn't even registered a point. Embarrassing for all concerned.)

But most of the time, and for most of the players, it gets a little tricky. If I have watched a particular team week in and week out, then it becomes easier for me to pick out who has had a good game and who hasn't. I learn to recognise individual players on the ice much quicker, and get used to the roles they have to play, but if you then asked me which player on the opposing team had had a good game then there would be a reasonable chance that I would go, 'Huh?' and shrug my shoulders stupidly. I suspect I am not alone in this, if the number of bizarre man of the match nominations is anything to go by. However, there are some people – who perhaps have a better intuitive understanding of the game than I have – who are able to spot good players much quicker than I can. This is frustrating. Refusing to believe that they could possibly be more intelligent than I am, I have often wondered if the ability to spot talent is a talent in itself.

'For me, it's real easy to see the skill players,' explains Kleinendorst. 'All you've got to do is watch Stefan Ketola and Jeff Tomlinson on the first day of practice, and you know that they are special players – offensively. That's obvious. But to learn which ones are special defensively actually takes a little bit of time. I mean, that doesn't come as easy as the offensive part of it. How they react to defensive situations, how they control plays down low, how they pin guys, how they don't let guys beat them back to the net. I mean, there are some guys who are very good offensively, but who are just *anaemic* defensively. To me, the trade-off just isn't worth it. I want someone who is more in balance. I'll take a guy who is not quite as good offensively, but pretty good defensively, and I think through that, you get a better balance.' But is this ability to spot the weaknesses in a player's game something that you are born with or is it something that you develop over a period of time?

'I think that it takes time. You know, I mean, like I was saying, that part doesn't come as easy as the offensive part. I think it takes a little bit of time to study your players, or study a player to see how he is defensively.' So could you tell a good player from just one game, I wondered. More than that, could you spot a guy who was a good player, but who in the particular match you were watching, was having a bad game? 'I think so, for sure,' feels Kurt. 'I would say a lot of it is going to depend on the skill level. Like if he's just a sloppy player – you know, a guy who's not pretty, if he's a sloppy player having a rough night, you know, then it's not going to be as easy to discover that player as it would be a gifted player, say for example, even a Kevin Hoffman. You know, a Kevin Hoffman having a rough night, I think you would still notice the potential in him because he's pretty solid in a lot of areas. It all depends on the player's skill level. And from there it goes.'

Of course, choosing hockey players isn't as simple as walking into an exclusive restaurant and picking the lobster you want from the fish tank ('I'll have *that* one, please'). Whilst players, like the lobster, may have strong opinions about where they are going to end up, hockey players tend to have the advantage of having some some say in the matter. After spending the last few seasons trying to get players to sign on the dotted line for teams in the ECHL, I wondered how easy Kurt found it was to get guys to come over to Britain, where, presumably, most of them hadn't even realised hockey was played. 'It's easy. It's not hard to recruit players here. This league is getting a better and better reputation. It's going to keep getting better as long as the league will allow it to get better. So it's not very difficult to talk to players, I don't even have to recruit. I really don't.'

This is not to say that Eric Lindros will soon be scrambling to join Basingstoke, but the quality of player coming to Britain is improving all the time. Whereas, before, the drop in playing standard from the NHL to the British game used to be so vertiginous that top players would inevitably look elsewhere in Europe to play, it now seems that Britain is becoming a little more alluring. 'It's excellent hockey. You're treated very well,' Darryl Olsen said when asked about his impressions of the British game after spending a season in Nottingham. 'I've played in Italy, and I think British ice hockey is like the hidden secret right now. Once a lot of players back home get wind of this, you're going to see a lot of great hockey players coming over here.'

The main reason for this, of course, is moolah. 'I've recruited for the last five years, and I've had to try to get guys to play for me for about £150 a week (probably less than a third of what the typical Superleague player gets),' says Kleinendorst. 'These guys do well enough here that, you know, when it comes time that they know they are not going to make it back home, and they have the choice of staying back there and bussing around the American league, or coming over here, we're going to get them here. Because, actually, the money that we pay them is substantially more than what they can make in the American league.'

However, just because a player may have decided to play in Europe doesn't mean that he will settle on Britain. The top league in Germany, the DEL, is probably the most lucrative league for players outside the NHL, with some Swiss clubs also offering their imports a lot of money. Surprisingly, though, Kleinendorst doesn't worry about losing players to other European leagues. 'Well, we don't compete. There's not much going on in Sweden and Finland for imports, each team gets a couple. So we're not in competition with those leagues at all. And we are really not in that much competition with the DEL, except for their middle-of-the-line players. Not the top players, not the bottom players, the players in the middle. Guys like Tomlinson, Ketola, and Davie Morrison.'

Presumably, if the money is about the same, the thing that will swing it in favour of playing in Britain is the language.

Hockey players aren't generally renowned for their ability to adapt to new languages and cultures. 'Yeah, that's a big advantage. I think that's a big plus,' admits Kleinendorst. 'That's why Davie Morrison is here. I mean, Jeff Tomlinson, he learnt German, and he spoke very good German, but being a Canadian . . . This league compares somewhere between the DEL and the German first division. So it's a better league than what Tomlinson and Ketola were playing in last year, and the facility is just second to none.'

Another attraction for players is the fans. I once sat next to a Finnish ice hockey journalist at a Storm game against Bracknell. Knowing he had watched hockey all over Europe, I was keen to gain his impressions of what he had seen. Whilst he had been impressed by the quality of the hockey, what had really taken him aback was the extent to which the fans had got involved. 'These fans are very good. I would think only in Cologne, have I ever seen noisier fans.' This struck me as odd, as the crowd on that particular night were probably less boisterous than usual. When I told Kleinendorst this he wasn't surprised that the journalist had spoken so highly of the crowd. 'The fans here are wonderful. I mean, really, there's no group of fans anywhere that compare to these. This is the best I've ever seen. From an overall fan standpoint – being supportive of the players, being enthusiastic for the game, enjoying the moment, having fun, these are the best.' His sentiment is genuine.

Telford player Martin Smith once told me that the biggest difference between fans in Britain and North America was that they were so appreciative here. They were fans rather than critics. Anyone who has ever been to the Cathedral Arches in Manchester after a game will have seen that the players are often mobbed by adoring fans. For some players, this attention can come as a bit of a culture shock. 'We get some guys who don't appreciate that sort of thing,' admits Kleinendorst, 'but we've got a group of guys that do. They're good about it. They're good with the kids. They're good looking guys...' Ah. There is that too. The sex appeal. There are many stories, probably apocryphal, of teenage girls, hockey players, and toilet cubicles.

Why any girl would prefer to flirt with a rugged, beaten up hockey player, as opposed to a bespectacled hockey writer, for instance, is beyond me, but knowing that Storm players are almost as likely to be asked to autograph underwear as programmes, I wondered if any of the adulation bothered Kleinendorst. Was he concerned that it might go to their heads?

'Nah, I don't think so. 'Cos then we come in here and play Nottingham and get whacked back down to size. The league is good about that. But I think it's good that they feel special about themselves. Because when they feel special, they play like they're special.'

So really, given the money, facilities, organisation and attention that these players get, it was perhaps no surprise that Kleinendorst found it so easy to recruit them. They wanted to come. 'Who wouldn't, I mean, that's the thing,' he says. 'Take a look around. I know we've got guys in that locker room that maybe won't be invited back next year, that are just going to kick themselves in the rear, and say "Why? Why did I let this happen?" If you're not going to make it in the NHL, and you're not going to make it in the DEL, why wouldn't you do everything you could possibly do to stay here? And make this work. And help this team . . .'

So, assuming you've scouted thoroughly, and decided which players you want for your team, and then persuaded them to sign, you might think that the hard work is done. Not a bit of it. More difficult than simply spotting good players is actually getting along with them once you've installed them in your team. In addition to the jobs of psychologist, who motivates the team, talent spotter, who recruits the players, and strategist, who plots how the team is going to play, it's now time to get out the lab coat because there is another area that a coach needs to look at – team chemistry. Obviously, no team is ever going to be successful unless it has the right blend of players. Small players need big players to protect them. Big players need the speed of small players to open up the ice. Young players need veterans to look up to, whilst older players need the invigorating presence of young players to get excited and motivated themselves. Leaders need others to inspire, and players need leaders to follow. But more than that, team chemistry extends beyond the physical attributes and skills of the players. It is just as important in terms of bonding. Of getting along with each other. A lot of the time it is difficult for outside observers to really appreciate team chemistry. You may even have a guy on a team who seems to be of only peripheral importance on the ice, but is in fact crucial to a team because of what he brings to it off the ice. Some players earn their money in the dressing room, as well as on the ice. This can be very hard to appreciate, and often removing a player from a team can unsettle team chemistry in ways which couldn't have been anticipated.

Publicly, Kleinendorst went on record several times during his first season in Britain saying that he 'liked his team'. Choosing to take him literally, I asked him if it was possible to have players in his team who, whilst they may be fine players, may not be so fine in their personalities off the ice. Could you tolerate someone in your team who you actually disliked on a personal level? 'You have to,' was his honest response. 'Especially here, you know. Not every player in that locker room has been a person that, you know, I really thought I was getting. I haven't missed by much, but all it takes is a couple of those guys and it can disrupt the whole chemistry of what we've got here. I mean, I've always tried to work it out with a player. I would always do these one-on-one meetings, I would always let him know my concerns. I would always let him know I held nothing against him. I want that guy to be a good person, but the only thing I really care about is to win, when all is said and done. I can deal with a guy who maybe has a different personality, as long as we could continue to win and he's not a disruption. Once he starts taking away from your locker room, and your team chemistry – Zero Tolerance. I mean, he's got to go. If he's a disruption in the dressing room then you gotta get rid of him.' True to his word, Kurt was later to release Jim Hrivnak from his contract, not because of his failings on the ice, far from it, but because of the amount of discord with the netminder in the dressing room.

In North America it is easier for coaches to deal with difficult personalities. In the NHL, an awkward player can be traded, or sent down to the minors. Here in Britain, players very rarely change teams mid season, and unless you are talking about the young girls who sometimes follow ice hockey players around (puck-bunnies) there are no minors. For someone used to the North American way of doing things, it has taken a bit of an adjustment, and when Kurt found that he had an off-ice problem with a certain player, he was frustrated by how little he could do. 'Normally there's something you can do about it, but here your hands are tied. I mean, there is something I can do about it, and that something is to send the kid home, but I've got to pay his contract, basically. That would be one thing that I wish we did better over here. That we didn't give them guaranteed contracts. So this league really ties a coach's hands when it comes to that kind of a situation. Whereas back home I had no time, here, you can't trade the guy. So the answer to your original question is, depending on the degree of what you're talking about, the coach has to tolerate it.'

Whilst this might give the impression that Kleinendorst has to endure some unpleasant characters in his team, he is at pains to stress that not every guy who pulls on a team sweater is obnoxious. In fact, he likes them. 'I do. I mean, I really do like everyone in my locker room. I really do,' he insists. 'Now, do I like some of them better than others when it comes to how they play? Absolutely. Do I like some of them better than others when it comes to how they are as people? Sure. I got some great guys in there who would go through the wall for me. You know, likewise, I would do the same for them. Then I've got some other guys . . . ' Some other guys that would first want a close look at that wall? And then maybe some time to sleep on it before deciding whether or not they wanted to run into it? 'Yeah. But I understand that. So I can't let that affect how I feel about them because it's not fair to the team. As long as they contribute, and they can help us win, and they are not a distraction, then I need to find a way to make it work.'

With the dawn of all-import hockey, and the all but total

annihilation of youth development for Superleague teams, there has been another shift in emphasis for British coaches. No longer do coaches think so much along the lines of blooding new talent so that, a few seasons down the line, they will reap the rewards. Nowadays, it is much more a question of bringing in players good enough for you to be up and running from day one. Whilst this short-termism isn't necessarily the fault of the coaches, after all, they know that if they don't deliver on the ice, regardless of what they do off it, they will be sacked, it is hardly conducive to developing good British talent. Tony Hand, for example, was flung into the Murrayfield Racers first team at 15 years old, and more recently, Stevie Lyle was just 14 when he first stepped into the Cardiff goal. Whilst both these players were exceptional talents, it is highly unlikely that either would have got the same kind of opportunity to play top flight hockey in Britain today. Aware of this problem, and whilst not pretending that it is the perfect solution, Kleinendorst has a North American idea that he feels would be a good idea to implement in Britain.

'In fact we are proposing something for next year that I think would help British hockey, which is the farm team system,' he explains. 'I would like the Superleague, and even the BIHA, to allow every one of our Superleague teams an additional four players on their roster. Four young players who have British stamps in their passports, and who, for example, Manchester could send to Blackburn. And these players would practise with us every day. They would practise with Blackburn, whenever Blackburn practised. They would play their games with Blackburn. Then, when I have injuries, or if one of those players develops to a point where I like them, we would call them up and they would play with us. So very similar to what you have back in the NHL, but on a level of only four players. And what it does is it helps their league, because it's going to bring in four players of good calibre, and it's going to help British ice hockey, because they would be British. They'd get practice sessions here with us, which should improve their game. I tried to do it before this season, but there wasn't the time.'

There was also likely to be some hesitancy on the part of the clubs who would act as farm teams. 'It seems to me that some of the problems we are going to run into are that the teams we would like to be associated with are a little sceptical about our intentions, and that just creates a few more headaches,' he admits. 'Basically, it sounds to me like they want to have their cake and eat it too. They want us to help them get their players, which is the way I see it too. I see us as being a really good contact for some of those teams to help them come up with three or four players who can help develop the British pool, actually subsidising them, to a certain extent, financially. But then when I need a player or two, I would have to be able to have the luxury of pulling that player out. That's what they are scared about. They might be a little cautious, because what they don't want to have happen is a situation where they have a big series of games coming up, and then a Superleague club calls up and says, "Hey, we need a goalie and a defenceman". Next thing you know they're without two players. But there's got to be a formula that we could put together that would work for everybody. Say you can only pull one player out at a time or whatever. I'm sure we can work it out. It's got to work both ways. They have to trust us, and believe that we are actually trying to do some good for them as well.'

Although a difficult concept for most British sports fans to get their heads around, the farm system is one widely used and accepted in North America. 'That's the concept they use back home, and it makes a lot of sense,' says Kurt. 'I really believe that there's nothing wrong with studying successful programmes, and I don't think anyone would argue that the NHL is the premier ice hockey league in the world. So why not take some of their ideas, and copy them, and help make our league a better league? To me, it almost looks like a win, win, win, win for everybody, so I don't understand why we couldn't make it work.' And to an extent, it *has* to work. Long term, the future of the sport is going to depend on a supply of domestic talent. At the moment the top level of the game is pulling away from the game at the grassroots level, but perhaps the farm system could help to bridge that gap. In a few years, we could start to see a generation of young British players making their mark in the same way that players like Tony Hand and the Coopers did in the earlier days of the Heineken League. It's certainly something Kleinendorst would love to see.

'I see everybody's point about British players,' he accepts. 'I agree with you, 100 per cent. Maybe, right now, the Superleague is a little too far advanced for a number of the good, young, British players – but they're there. There's got to be a way to help develop those young British players, so that in a year or two, or three, they're ready to jump into our league. Whereas right now, they aren't. And what they need is quality coaching. They need more ice time. And they need an opportunity. Well, they could get the quality coaching by being associated with a Superleague team in practices. They could get the game experience that they need by playing at the lower level, and then even another experience if we call them up to this level. So I don't see the downside to that at all. It would cover everybody's bases, and we would help develop a British pool of talent.' In theory, with improved standards of coaching, and a better standard of league to aim for, the British players that emerge in the future should be of a better calibre than ever.

And of course this notion of the farm team can work the other way too. Just as smaller British clubs can feed Superleague clubs, so might the Superleague start to feed the NHL. As the standard in the Superleague has risen, so has the possibility that British clubs could provide a farm club service for young European players on the way to the NHL. The fact that the Los Angeles Kings will be funding the new London franchise obviously suggests that NHL clubs and Superleague teams can start to work together, and the Manchester Storm are not alone in the Superleague in building up a working relationship with an NHL club, in this case the Ottawa Senators. In the future, is it not possible that young European talent might be interested in playing in the Superleague – which after all, is closer in playing style to North America than many European leagues – before making the step to playing in the NHL?

'Well, that's something I have put some thought into,' says Kurt. 'I think it would be useful, not just with Ottawa, but with any NHL club that has younger players coming out of Europe.' There are certainly benefits from the Superleague clubs' points of view. 'Financially, it makes sense, because you wouldn't have to step in and pay the whole player's salary – usually the other team will share in that. I think if [an NHL team] has some young players in Europe who wouldn't need work permits, then they would want to put them into a situation like this, in a developmental stage, as depth players, and we could get them on the cheap, which is always a factor – though these are just thoughts, I'm just thinking out loud. I would like to have a couple of young Ottawa Senators players here next year, to help me form, possibly, a fourth line. Good young kids, with good backgrounds, who have been drafted and that Ottawa has an interest in. Hopefully they would look at me as a coach who could help develop their young players. So that maybe the following year, those young players would have, basically, one full professional season under their belts, in a good programme, and then they can make the jump over the water, and fit in the AHL, or IHL, whatever. That's the vision I have got. I don't know if that will come around.'

And even if such a farm system doesn't fully arise, Kurt still feels the British game can benefit from contact with North American teams. Obviously, the game here is heavily influenced by the kind of players that come into the league, and Kurt has found that the Senators are only too happy to help with the homework when it comes to recruiting players to play here. 'Any time I get a player's name across my desk, whether I'm familiar with the player or not, I just put a fax into Roy Mlakar, who's the president of the Senators – he's kind of my contact person, and then he takes that particular player and he will send that player's name to whoever he feels will best know that player. So what comes back to me is a nice, detailed list of that player's strengths, that player's weaknesses, that player's personality, his character – which is really a nice thing for me to have. And we use that quite a bit. They've got scouts all over the world. There's no place that they don't have a scout, so any name that I send to them, they can get a background check for me.'

Talking to Kleinendorst, it is clear that he thinks about the game deeply. As we wound down the interview, I wondered if he was ever able to switch off from it when he went home and just turn his mind to other things. His answer was emphatic. 'Never, never, *never*,' he replied, shaking his head and saying 'never' even as I was asking the question. In fact, I had to edit a few 'nevers' out. He is, quite definitely, very clear on this point. 'It's unbelievable,' he says. 'That's the frustrating part about it. Like honestly. *Never*. When I leave here at night, there's always something going through my head. When I'm at home, honestly, I mean, I really work hard. I love my family to death. Family comes first. But I'm telling you, I'm sitting at home at the dinner table and I'm enjoying my family, but there's always stuff going through my head, you know?' In that case, does he ever wish he *could* just switch off and leave his brain off the hook for a few minutes?

'I love hockey. Always have,' he replied with happy resignation, as if the possibility of being able to switch off was so remote that there was no point even thinking about it. 'Even when I was a player it was the same way. You know. Even in the summer. I just love what I'm doing. I'm one of those fortunate guys who was able to continue on with his first love. And you would have to have grown up where I did to really appreciate why I'm the way I am. I grew up in a town that was just crazy for hockey. I idolised their hockey players. And from there it just kept going. Even in the summer, when I find time to enjoy myself way, way more, I still think about it a lot. But, being in this position here, I can't turn it off. 'Cos every morning, even last summer, every single morning I was up on the telephone. What I would try to do would be to get up while my family was still in the rack, and do what I could get done in a few hours so that during the day we could spend time together. But that's when I can find more time to turn it off.'

Given this state of affairs, I decided to venture further into

Kleinendorst's psyche. Somewhat foolishly, I told him that I even dreamt about hockey sometimes, and, erm, wondered if he did the same. Evidently, I had gone too far, even for him. 'I'm not a bad sleeper,' he replied, laughing. 'I think it's probably because of what you're talking about. When I go to bed, I mean, I'm out. I have a very clean conscience. Ethically, nothing would keep me from sleeping. I think because all day your head is constantly turning these thoughts, that I just think I'm pretty pooped at the end of the day, and I just go right to sleep.' Aah, good. Just asking, you know.

A reporter once asked Alex Ferguson about how long he was able to savour the moment of victory and triumph. To this guy's surprise, Ferguson claimed that the euphoria he felt at winning was very transitory. That after just a few moments it was gone. He wasn't driven by the need to experience it. He was driven simply because it was in his nature to be driven. The satisfaction came not in reaching his goal, but in travelling towards it. Given that Kleinendorst seems equally consumed by his chosen sport, I asked him where his moment of satisfaction came. 'You know, I'll tell you. Really, you know, there's not a nicer feeling than walking off the ice after your team has just won a game. And you've basically seen things that as a group you've put together – that they've executed, that they've done a nice job. The fans are screaming, the music's blaring. There's not a better feeling in the world. I mean, really. It's really good. And then you come in. And enjoy it for a little bit. And then start thinking about the next night. That's what it is.'

Whilst this made sense to me, I couldn't help notice that it contrasted with my own pattern of enjoyment, and that of most other fans. For us, it is the game itself, rather than its aftermath, that provides us with our highest highs and our lowest lows. Whilst the moment the final hooter sounds to secure victory is undoubtedly sweet, and we can probably still enjoy the buzz of the win for days, sometimes it is the actual instant the winning goal is scored, or the moment the big save is made that provides us with our moments of delirium or anguish. The coach, perhaps by necessity, has to be a lot more reserved during the actual game, suppressing his emotions until the outcome is known. Not allowing himself to be swept along by a game in the way that spectators, and for that matter, players do. Was there never any point that a coach could enjoy whilst the game was still in progress? After a few moments in thought, Kurt allowed himself to acknowledge one. 'The other night. [A table-topping game against Ayr, won 5–3.] The game was in the bag, and there was a break in the play with a few minutes to go, and the music was playing, and it was that one song that they play when we're going to win [Bryan Adams' 'We're gonna win', surprisingly enough], I guess, and the fans get up, and that's a . . . that's a pretty nice feeling . . . Right there.'

Yeah . . . Yeah, it is.

The Great Randino

Undoubtedly, one of the great tragedies of life on this planet has been the creeping realisation that I am probably never going to make it as a professional ice hockey player. Whilst there are still some guys playing who are older than me, I am now 29 years old, and my years of devotion to the couch-potato lifestyle have probably robbed me of the blistering pace I once had. A bad football injury I sustained when I was younger has left me with a dodgy knee, and being ruthlessly honest, I would probably stand a better chance of making it if I knew how to skate. But still I dream. I still imagine that I might one day awaken to find that I have inexplicably been blessed with the hockey prowess of Mario Lemieux. That I then get the call from a desperate head coach on the eve of the big game whose team are up against it, who've got an unexpected opening on their roster and who are willing to give me a last shot at the big time . . . But then I come back to reality. It is a foolish fantasy. It will never happen. We all know that players have to be registered with the league before they can play – they'd never get the paperwork in on time.

But it's a nice dream. To be a hockey player. To play the game. To live the life. Yet I often get the impression from players when I talk to them that most of the guys who do get to do it, take it for granted. It's not really surprising, after all, very few of us ever appreciate the things in life we have. We only have one life, and with no other life to make comparisons with, it naturally becomes more difficult to be grateful for everything in it. It is only because my own mundane, cruddy life seems so boring compared to that of a hockey player that my fantasy of being one is so alluring. And yet, if something hideous were to befall me, then chances are I'd suddenly appreciate this life much more. As the renowned Canadian philosopher, Joni Mitchell, once pointed out, don't it always seem as though we don't know what we've got 'til it's gone? A point, I'm certain, not lost on her fellow Canadian Randy Smith. Randy Smith is a hockey player – but because of something that happened to him, he doesn't take anything for granted.

Born in Saskatoon, Canada, in 1965, Randy was actually quite a fine hockey player. Like most Canadian kids, he dreamt of playing in the NHL, but unlike most, he actually made it to the big league after being drafted by the Minnesota North Stars. Unfortunately, he wasn't able to build a career there, but he was still good enough to represent Canada in the World Championships and even picked up a silver medal in the 1992 Winter Olympics. He then had a couple of spells playing in Europe, first in Switzerland, then Austria, before finding himself back in North America when he played in the International Hockey League for Las Vegas Thunder in their inaugural season.

'I was trying to get a job and stay in North America,' he recalls, 'and it was late August and I got a call from the Las Vegas GM and he said, "We're willing to sign you, but you're not going to play a whole lot. You're going to be our fourth line centre. You're going to be a checker – you might kill the odd penalty, whatever, but that's what you're going to be." So I took it, because I wanted to stay in North America.' Unfortunately, it was to be a difficult year. 'I didn't really have that good a season. I was put on a checking line, and I just didn't have the stats at the end to warrant another year.' For Smith, the problem wasn't so much having to play a more defensive role than he was used to – after all, if it was what the team needed then he was happy to do it – but it was the fact that this defensive role wasn't taken into account when the time came to renew contracts.

'If you're an offensive player put into a different role they still want to see those stats. They say, "Well, we realise you were just checking against the other team's centre, or playing against their top line, but why didn't you still score? Sorry, we can't give you a job now because you didn't do that." That was the position I was put in. If you're a defensive player, no one comes up to you and says, "You did a really good job checking, but how come you didn't score those three goals?" It doesn't really make sense to me that kind of thinking. Then after that year, having been an offensive player my whole career, other teams went "Gee, look, he only got 20 points. He's obviously through. He doesn't have it anymore."' And so Smith was out of a job. Was he annoyed? 'I wouldn't say annoyed. I was professional enough to know that if that's what they wanted me to do then that's what I had to do. But I would have liked to have been given a broader job, to show my strength.'

And so Smith found himself at a bit of a crossroads. He was 29, which in hockey terms is by no means old, but a lot of the teams outside the NHL are very much geared up to developing new talent, and he certainly didn't qualify as that. Faced with grinding out his career as a role player in North America he recalled his experiences in Europe and decided to look overseas again, something that a lot of his peers did. 'I think with a lot of the guys, it just gets to be the age,' he feels. 'Over here you get to play a lot longer. Obviously, the really good older players are playing in the NHL, and the minor teams will keep some of the older guys around for experience, but a lot of the minor league teams are filled with the young up-and-coming players, so I think that's why a lot of guys turn to Europe. There's lots of guys who are still very much capable of playing back home who still come over here. A lot choose to be over here because they can extend their careers a lot.

'You have your choice. I mean you could stay in North America and do that same old routine. It's pretty much the same grind every day – bus, hotel, game, practice . . . bus, hotel, game, practice. Or you could come over here and see a part of the world that a lot of the guys would probably never get a chance to see, if it weren't for the hockey.' And so at the start of the 1994/95 season Smith headed for Britain to play for the Premier Division Peterborough Pirates. He admits that looking back, it was pretty much a step into the unknown, and what little he had known of British hockey hadn't exactly made it sound like the most enticing place to play. 'I knew Ross and Dale Lambert, who are my teammates now and are from Saskatoon, and I'd heard them tell stories, like, seven or eight years ago, "Oh yeah, then we beat Medway 21–2, and I had 14 goals and six assists . . . ' and I thought like, "What have I got myself into?" But then I got here and it wasn't as bad as I was originally expecting.' Having said that, it was still a far cry from the Superleague.

'It was nowhere near what it is now,' admits Smith. 'The hockey was bad, four years ago. There were basically just the imports, the top British players, and then a lot of the other guys were just there for . . . I don't want to say things that are going to make them look bad, I mean, they had other jobs, but I'm playing with guys who are bricklayers during the day, and then who have to come to the rink. I mean, there's no way I could have done that and then given it my best effort. I always appreciated the effort they put in because of the fact that this wasn't their career, this was just something they were doing because they loved the game, but there wasn't a lot of talent. The talent was spread thin, and some teams grabbed all the best ones.' For a player of Smith's quality, surely he must have been a little bit disappointed. 'I *was* disappointed,' he admits. 'I mean, I had played in the Olympics, the World Championships, and then all of a sudden, here I am . . . ' Here he was indeed. In his first game, against Cardiff, he saw his side go down 17–3. In the home opener, also against Cardiff, it was 10–10. This was clearly a different standard of hockey than what he was used to.

'I mean it was fun for a while. I used to be able to phone home and tell my parents, or my buddies, "Yeah, I got seven goals last night." But that wore off, after a while. It wasn't fun. Getting seven goals wasn't that good, I *should* have been capable of getting those seven goals, and if I didn't get seven, or whatever number it was, then I should have been disappointed.' Looking back on some of those unlikely scorelines, it's no wonder that Smith felt it was a bit of a culture shock. 'Anyone who knew about hockey would just say, "Then the hockey's obviously brutal." Because there's no way anyone can score five goals a game consistently. You might be able to do it once every season, but guys getting seven, eight, nine points a game, every game – then the hockey is obviously not that good. For the hockey to be up where it is now, compared to how it was when I arrived, I would have never ever believed that could happen.'

Despite dropping down so far to play in Britain, Smith still felt he had a job to do. While many guys in his position would have just taken one look at the standard of the league and then jumped on the first plane back home, Smith decided to give it his best shot. The results were spectacular. In his 60 games for the club he scored 104 goals, and racked up 106 assists. He was then elected to the Premier Division All Star team, was voted the league's Player of the Year by the British Ice Hockey Writers Association and was also voted the Player's Player of the Year. To cap all of this, and much to his own astonishment, he was then invited back into the Team Canada fold to tour Europe at the end of the season. 'That was something that I never expected,' he recalls, not unreasonably, considering that no one playing in the wilderness of British hockey had ever been bestowed that particular honour before. Startling though his form had been throughout the season, his inclusion on the party probably owed more to the fact he had actually played against Team Canada when they played an exhibition game against the Pirates that year, and had done very well on a night when Peterborough, with more ringers than a campanologist convention, had stunned Team Canada.

'We somehow beat them – I've no idea how – 3–2. And I scored a goal, got a couple of assists, and I got an assist the next night when we lost 5–1. And they mentioned to me after the game that they'd be getting a squad together and invited me to come. So at the end of the season I went to a mini training camp in Czechoslovakia. Played two games, scored a goal in the second match, was made man of the match – and they released me right after that game . . . kind of surprised me. I think they had just needed a roster of guys for those two games. I think from that group of about 30 guys, only two stayed on.' Despite this slight knockback, there was no doubt that Smith had made a tremendous impact in his debut season here. By general consensus, he was the best import in Britain. What had made all this even more amazing was the fact that the Pirates team he had joined that year were not a particularly good side. With few other quality players to draw upon, they had relied heavily upon him, and there was no doubt that for Smith the whole experience had been a bit of an eye–opener.

In Las Vegas he had been only a small part of the team's offence. In Peterborough, he *was* the offence. 'Well, I liked that. Regardless of where I'm playing, I like to be the guy that the team is counting on. Whether I am or not, I try to tell myself that I'm the guy that has to do it. I knew in Peterborough that if I didn't score three or four goals, we had no chance of winning whatsoever. And I liked that. I think a lot of guys come over here and they get complacent. They just think, "Sure, I need to score five, but they'll be happy with two . . . " – I think there've been a lot of good players here that aren't here any more because of that attitude – "I know I can get 80 goals this year, but if I get 60, they'll be happy and have me back." I took the attitude that if they wanted me to get 60 to come back, I'd try to get 90 . . . to make *sure* they wanted me back. I like being the guy that the team, the management, and everybody counts on.'

And of course, Peterborough did count on him. There have been few occasions in Britain where one player has so obviously carried a team, and Smith relished the challenge. 'We had Dale Jago, Brent Bobyck, Jeff Lyndsay, all really good players – but two of them were defencemen, and you can't expect them to get five goals a game, regardless of them being imports, and Brent was hurt a lot of the season. So I really did feel that if we were going to win any games it was going to have to be me who scored the goals. And I'm not saying that it was me who scored the goals by myself. All the guys, everyone, the British guys, they were a huge part of my success. I mean, they'd go into the corner, and get a stick in the face, and an elbow on the back of the head, and then get cross-checked into the ice but still manage to flip the puck out to me, and I'd put it in the net and so look like the big hero. But I've always appreciated the effort the other players, including the British guys, made.'

With the team often crippled by injuries to their other key players the Pirates found that they had inadvertently introduced a new playing system to British hockey, a new tactic called 'Give the puck to Randy'. It might have been as subtle as a breeze block in the face, but it kept them in most of the games. Smith recalls the pre-match briefings: 'A lot of the game plan was, "Uh, Joe, you get the puck, find Randy, give it to him. And if he can't beat two or three guys, and he does happen to give it back to you, then give it right back."' Smith, too, would have his own instructions. 'We used to come in before the game, and Cam (Plante, the player-coach) would say to me "Okay, like go out there, and unless you absolutely have to, don't come off." And he'd have the lines drawn up on the board, it would be like "Joe, Randy, Pete" then "Tom, Randy, Tim", "Cam, Randy, Dale . . . " It got to me. I mean it was funny. I'd come in and see myself on all three lines . . . ' Oh well, at least it meant a lot of ice time. 'Yeah. There was one weekend, in particular, when I went through both games and *never* came off. And I woke up Monday and I felt like I was 59, not 29. But then that was fun too. I mean any player, in any sport, wants to play as much as they can.'

With Smith working so tirelessly for the cause, the Pirates fans were quick to show their devotion, much to his bemusement. 'It was fun. I came from North America, where I don't think they idolise players the way they do here. I mean, I went from being a guy on the team, to coming to Peterborough, where the crowd were singing songs about me. It was just bizarre. I think I was embarrassed to start with, but then I realised that they truly meant it. They were really good hockey fans in Peterborough. I mean, I don't think they'd enjoyed a whole lot of success, as a team. They did have some good players, but they saw that maybe I was going to be a good player and they really appreciated that. And it was genuine. It wasn't like, "Oh well, let's just fool around and sing a song." I really think it was genuine. And I enjoyed it because of that. The first time I heard it I thought "Oh my God" but then, after a while, it was nice . . . '

The fans in Peterborough, who could barely contain their glee at what a good player they had landed, certainly made an impression on Smith. At the risk of sounding corny, when he went out to play, he did it not only for himself and his teammates, but the fans too. 'No matter who you are, there's always games where you don't really feel up to par, or maybe you've got the flu, whatever, and you're thinking, "Lets get this over with," and then all of a sudden they'd be singing and cheering and stuff, and I mean, I'd think, "They're here, they've paid their money, I've got to do my job. I'm a scorer, so I'd better score because these people deserve to have me do my job." So it made it easy. I always wanted to go to the rink. Who wouldn't want to go to the rink when there's 2,000 people singing your name?'

Whilst Smith, to his own surprise, found that he was really enjoying his spell in Peterborough, and increasingly getting used to British hockey's various quirks, there was a blot looming on the horizon. An alien concept to North Americans, relegation was beckoning the Pirates. 'I'd never even heard of that before,' admits Smith, when he recalls his initial bafflement at the idea. 'I never heard of a team in one league finishing in a certain spot and then having to play teams from a lower division to see if they could remain in the top league or not. That was something that was totally new. I learnt about that when I arrived, that there was a possibility that that could happen, so everyone had to try to get themselves together so that that didn't happen – unfortunately we didn't, so that was the end of that.'

At the end of the relegation play-offs the Pirates had missed out on staying up by a single goal (Slough pipping them on goal difference with a goal scored in the last 15 seconds of the final game of the season – ouch), and Smith knew his spell in Peterborough was over. Had they not fallen, would he have stayed? 'I would say there would have been a really good chance, yeah. I've talked to the directors since, and they understood my situation totally. I let it be known right away that if we were relegated then there probably would be no chance that I'd be back. I wanted to play the very best hockey available to me, and when I came here and first saw what the hockey was, I thought, "Well, I'm not even sure *this* is going to cut it." And then to be dropped down *another* division, well, there would have just been no way I could have done it.'

Of course, after a season like the one he had just had, it was no surprise when the Cardiff Devils moved quickly to sign him, and whilst he had very much enjoyed his time in Peterborough there was no doubt that he had joined a more professional club. 'I'll never say anything bad about the directors in Peterborough, but they were just four businessmen who wanted to see hockey in Peterborough – and they did a very good job running it. But when I moved to Cardiff it was more business-like. I mean, I'm not even sure I had a contract signed in Peterborough. For whatever reason, we didn't get around to it, though I never thought for one moment that I wouldn't get my money. They were genuinely nice people, and I think they appreciated what I was doing.' They also appreciated what good value for money Smith had been. Unlike many players coming into the league now, he had taken a fair drop in salary to come to Britain in the first place. Something he had always been realistic about.

'I think, like a lot of guys, when you first come over to Britain you can't command some big, huge salary. Partly, because a lot of the teams didn't have a lot of money to start with and, I think, four or five years ago, wouldn't have known how good you were anyway. They didn't really do a lot of checking up on you. I remember arriving in Peterborough and it said in the programme "Former NHL star for the Minnesota North Stars", and I remember thinking to myself "Well, they obviously didn't check and see that it was only three games, not 300 . . . ” So I think a lot of guys got here on their *own* word of mouth. Phoning up and saying “Hey, I’m good, I’m coming . . . ” So, the money was less, but I had to get here and make an impression so that I could make more.’

Naturally, the move to Cardiff also meant that he could make more. ‘I’m not going to lie, that was part of the reason in moving from Peterborough,’ admits Smith, obviously wary of the criticism that professional sportsmen attract when they change teams. ‘If you said to a guy who’s a painter, “Oh you’re making £10,000 now, you can come and paint in my company for £20,000,” then he’d probably be crazy not to go.’ Whilst this might seem blindingly obvious to most people, it could still be a bone of contention in some teams, especially where some players were earning substantially more than some of their teammates. As a full-time professional, Smith was obviously one of the ones paid more, and there was always the chance that this could cause resentment from some quarters.

‘That was hard – playing with guys who didn’t have to be there. It was a little bit of extra cash for them, though they obviously liked the game. Even when I went to Cardiff I was still playing with guys who worked. There would be the odd time, some animosity, some guy might say, “Well, gee, *I* don’t make that amount of money,” and so you’d almost feel bad about making the amount of money you did, compared to a 19-year-old British kid, working in a steel factory for £100 a week. But that’s the way it is. If someone’s good enough they’ll make the money. I mean, Tony Hand makes a lot of money, nobody says to him, “Well, you’re British. You can only make this amount.” He’s good enough, so he makes it.

‘A lot of people think athletes are going to change teams just because of money. I mean, if it’s a huge amount then somebody is going to leave. But if it’s £10 or £15 a week and they like where they are, they’re not going to leave for that amount of money. Had Peterborough not been relegated, I’m sure they’d have come up with some money somehow, perhaps not quite as much as I was going to get in Cardiff, but it would have been interesting to see what I would have done had they stayed in the Premier because I really enjoyed it there. I wouldn't rule out playing there again because my wife and I liked it there.'

For now though, he was in Cardiff, and after battling away for a struggling side it made a nice change to be involved with a team that would be a strong contender for the Championship. 'We did have a hard time winning games in Peterborough, but in Cardiff the team, fans, the management all expected to win, and wanted to win every game. It was a whole different atmosphere,' recalls Smith. For one thing, there was actually an acknowledgement of the tactical side of the game. 'I went from "Open the door and come back when you're tired . . . and if you're not tired, then I'll see you after the game," to Cardiff, where we had systems, guys had certain roles, maybe one line designed to be a little more offensive than others, then a defensive guy on the wing, whatever. It was back to actual systems. A lot of games were won on the system we played and not just on the talent we had, because other teams now had that same talent. Whereas in Peterborough it was get your talented guys out there, and hope they could last 59 minutes . . .'

In his first year with the Devils, Smith led the team in scoring, though the team itself was to have a frustrating year, finishing as runner-up in the league and missing out on the Wembley Championship for the first time in several years. By this stage, the standard of play had started to rise. 'We noticed a slight improvement,' remembers Smith, 'and then all the players heard talk of a Superleague, with no restrictions on imports, but we thought it was maybe some kind of a marketing ploy to get hockey noticed. And then all of a sudden, it *did* happen and the standard just went right up.' After years of fans being promised that it was just around the corner, three line hockey finally arrived. 'Even four lines almost,' enthuses Smith. 'Six defencemen, two very good goalies . . . Whereas when I first arrived it had been one line – and maybe not even a goalie. It's too bad to say, but there were some teams with goalies that weren't that good. I'd be surprised if there was anyone with an average of less than five or six [goals against] four years ago.

'Cos there were scores of 17–12. That was commonplace. It went from being a pretty good league, to a very good league, and I think it caught a lot of people off guard.'

The future looked bright, then. Smith had found himself a key player on a team that was poised for success in the new Superleague, and with another year of his contract to run he could look forward to an exciting season. However, there was a problem – niggling at first, but then quickly rather more serious, then finally out-and-out scary. The biggest fear of any professional athlete is to get injured, and throughout his career Smith had got his share of knocks like any other player. This time, though, it was different. 'My first year in Cardiff, I got hurt in February,' he recalls. 'There was one incident when I remember being hit, and then that's when I started noticing the back pain. They said if that's when it happened, then it was probably that, though it could just be a coincidence – maybe just 20 years of skating, and being hit into the boards. Or it just could be that it happened. It could happen to a guy who just sits at a desk all day. But there was one incident in Humberside or Milton Keynes, I believe, where I was hit, and I kind of got my top half twisted one way, then a guy fell into my legs and sent them the other way, and everything just kind of twisted. And that's when I first noticed the pain. I don't think they thought it was anything major. I think they just thought I'd maybe bruised something or other.'

Despite the discomfort, Smith continued to play through the injury. It is what hockey players do. Like most sportsmen, they find injuries frustrating, and would generally prefer to play hurt than not at all. Hockey, in particular, has a culture where it is almost expected that guys should battle through injury. Partly, this is attributable to the fact that there is a fair amount of machismo involved – hockey players enjoy their reputation for toughness, they are renowned for their ability to carry on playing with broken limbs and cracked heads, and to not play because of an injury can often be seen as weakness, or as putting yourself before the team, but partly it is also because of one of the peculiarities of the game. In football, for instance, when a player gets hurt, the team can replace him with a substitute, but in hockey, substitutes aren't used to replace injured players, they are used continuously as players tire and come on and off all the time. This means that when a guy gets injured the team suffers from being a man down for the rest of the game as they can't then call on someone sitting in the stands to get dressed and join the bench. Playing hurt, then, is simply what you do.

'Every player I know, well a lot of them, will conceal injuries,' reveals Smith. 'I think it's changing a little nowadays. Because there're so many bigger, stronger players, there are a lot more injuries now than there used to be. I think team doctors are a little more sympathetic than they used to be. Five or six years ago when I was playing in North America, if you went to a doctor and said "I think I broke my hand," they'd say "Well, put some ice on it and put this wrap on it. We've got two games this weekend. Get those over with, then let's look at it . . . " Now they are a little more concerned with getting guys healthy. Maybe realising that if they keep a guy out for three games and get him fixed, it's better than having him at 50 per cent for the next ten games, and then realising it is serious, and him being out for six months.' This was part of the problem for Smith though. No one knew it *was* serious.

Not wanting to let the team down, Smith saw out the rest of the season playing in considerable pain. He mentioned the injury to the team doctor, but no one appreciated the full extent of the problem. 'They weren't really too sure what it was, though there was obviously a problem with my back. Then it got bad enough that I started taking steroid injections to get rid of the pain so that I could continue playing.' Whilst this might sound callous, in fairness to Cardiff there were problems with Smith's back that he hadn't told them about. 'The whole lower back, the pain was bad, but it got so that it would just paralyse me. Like everything in my back would quit. Like I can remember lying down with my daughter one night, and then she fell asleep, and I had to wake her up to go and get my wife because she was hoovering and couldn't hear me yelling. I couldn't get off the bed. I couldn't even move.'

This was clearly not just a hockey problem. This was real spooky stuff. Smith admits he was scared by it. 'I lay there and thought "How am I ever going to get up?" It was like someone had a big vice on my back, and they slowly let it off so I was able to get up. But I couldn't get from like here to the end of the block without unbelievable pain. I think the pain was trying to tell me, "Okay, sit down and relax." But the pain got so bad, and I wasn't listening, it said, "Okay, if you're not going to listen, then I'll just shut you down." So everything would just seize right up and I couldn't even move.' To make matters worse, the timing was not good.

'We were getting ready for the play-offs when it first happened. How do you go and say, "Well, hold on guys, I've got some back pain?" I mean nobody would say it to your face, but a lot of guys would be like, "Hey, come on. It can't be that bad . . . " And I'm like my own worst enemy, whenever I get anything I never say a word.' So Smith played on without his teammates or the Devils really understanding what he was going through. Smith's point-per-game rating fell to about a third of what it had been, but with the Devil's season petering out anyway, it didn't attract too much criticism. The close season brought with it a chance to rest, and hopefully, for the injury to sort itself out. 'When I finished off the season I had groin surgery, and they said "Oh, this is like a blessing in disguise, now you can just relax for eight weeks and let your back heal. Rest should do it,"' remembers Smith.

'But as the eight weeks passed, it never ever got better. I came back, it was still really sore, and I played six games in the B&H Cup and it was absolutely . . . It was beyond a hockey injury now. I couldn't get on the floor to play with my daughter. I couldn't bend down to pick my new daughter out of her crib. I couldn't even get out of bed. It was like, literally, 20 minutes from waking up to actually sitting on the side of the bed.' Smith's anxiety and frustration at all of this was exacerbated by the fact that no one seemed to be able to work out what was wrong with him, which was disquieting in itself. 'Nobody was really saying, "Well, here's what's wrong with it . . . " It was like they weren't sure.' He remembers, 'They weren't finding any real evidence on the X-ray, or whatever tests they were doing. I'd come to physio and they'd say "move this way" or "move that way", and they'd say "Well, gee, that seems normal . . . there's obviously something not right but we're not sure what." And I had to ask how I could justify not playing when the doctors and the physios are saying "Well, we're not really sure what the matter is – if anything."'

To make this mess just that little bit more intolerable, fate had decided to introduce sod's law into the equation. 'It always seemed I'd not be able to move at home, and then get to the doctors – it's always the same no matter what I have, if I have a sore stomach, as soon as I get to the doctor, it's gone, so I'd get to physio and they'd say, "Do this . . . " and I'd be able to do it, and then an hour later, I'd be driving home, and then get home and wouldn't be able to get out of the car. And I'd be stuck there thinking, "Why didn't this happen, like an hour ago, so someone could have seen what this was actually like?" They did X-rays, and said, "Well look, there's nothing really wrong with it that we can see." And I'd say, "Okay, fine" and then go out to practise the next morning and two minutes into it I'd be lying on the ice not able to move.' It was an unbelievably frustrating time. 'There were nine months of not really knowing what was the matter with it, but knowing that if I did try and play that I wasn't going to be capable of doing the things I could usually do. I thought I had to get to the bottom of it, otherwise I'd be out there playing at 20 per cent of what I was capable of – those games I played in the B&H Cup, I was so badly hurt I was totally useless, and then they'd say, "Well, you're not good enough. So get out of here." It would be no use me saying, "But, but . . . ." because they'd say, "Well why didn't you tell us about your back before?"'

Whilst Smith was obviously worried about how the injury was going to affect his hockey career, his wife, sensitive to the amount of pain he was suffering, was looking to the big picture. This wasn't just about hockey any more. 'I couldn't live a normal day-to-day life. My wife said, "Use your head here. You're 31 years old, is this something that, when you're 41, you're going to be in a wheelchair? It's not worth going to Swindon to play in the Benson & Hedges Cup if it's going to cause problems ten years down the road.'" Smith was still uncertain of what to do, but increasingly, it seemed like this tough decision was being made for him by his body. 'It just got to a point where my body said "No. You can't do *anything*. Like *nothing*. You can't sit for more than two minutes, or else we'll stiffen up and you won't be able to move. So you decide if you want to get it fixed, or if you want to live like this." It wasn't "Should I or shouldn't I?" it was "I *have* to."'

After struggling for nine months with the injury without any kind of medical reassurance, it finally got too much for Smith. They weren't finding anything wrong with him and he was still expected to play. It was an intolerable situation. 'Finally, I went into Paul Heavey's office and said, "I really have got two choices, Paul. I have to retire, or something's got to be done. Because not only can I not play hockey but I can't walk. I can't play with my kids. I can't bend over." And he said, "Hey, I didn't realise it was this bad. Why didn't you say something?" I said, "Well, you were a player. You don't go every time and say I've got a bump on my elbow." I tried to make it clear that it was really bad, but I mean I didn't want to come across as some cry-baby, every day going in saying [whining voice] "My back hurts. My back hurts." Within minutes, he was on the phone, and from that point things started to move.'

Smith was quickly taken for a further series of tests, and to his considerable relief, this time the specialists did find out what the matter was. 'There was an MRI, a CAT scan – I've had so many tests on my back now that I can't even remember which took place when, but they came up with the fact that a disc had moved.' Like anyone who has a serious injury, Smith was to learn things about his body that he had never even considered before. 'There are joints called facet joints. Normally they don't move, but mine were because there was a space the disc had created, and they were basically just rubbing on the bone, and that was part of what was causing the pain. And the nerves were getting in there, and if a nerve got inside there and it moved, then it would clamp shut, and that was what was causing the lack of movement. Until that nerve moved back, I wouldn't be able to move. So the doctors said, "You can try and play, and come back in three months, and it might have settled – though the chances of that are small – or you can have the surgery." So my choices were, have the surgery and miss the season, or try going for another three or four months, probably have nothing fixed, and then have the surgery, miss that season, and probably the start of the next. So I – well, basically the doctor – decided there was no other option than to have the surgery. It wasn't going to get better on its own.' In order to decide whether to have the operation taken, Smith still had to know one thing. 'I had to know if I was going to be able to play hockey again after this. The doctor said, "Oh, yes. There's absolutely no problem. Probably not this year – though there's a small chance, but, yes."' The relief was immense.

Though he still had to face the surgery, Smith felt a lot of the stress fall away just because of the fact that they now knew what was wrong with him and others could now understand what he had been going through. 'Looking back, I don't think anyone was not sympathetic, but now it's all done with, I think people realise what a state I was in. It's hard to say, "My back's killing me. I can't move." But unless you've actually been there, and felt what the pain was like, to feel what it is like to lie in your bed and not actually be able to move, then you can't really understand it. I think before, if someone had come up to me and said, "Oh gee, my back's killing me . . ." I would probably have said, "Oh yeah? That's too bad . . ." but thought to myself, "Gee, how bad can it be?" But I think a lot of people now say "How's your back?" and I say, "Well it's good. Considering I've got like two screws and a metal disc in there." And they go, "Oh, jeez. That must have been something . . . They wouldn't have done that if it had just been a little bit of pain." So I think people realise now what I was going through.'

As the Devils got their first Superleague campaign under way,

Smith went into hospital. It was to be no picnic. 'I had the surgery on 15 October and then they put me into like a body brace, from just below my waist to almost under my chin. And I had that on for ten weeks. I was only allowed to take it off to shower. That basically kept my upper body totally straight. There was absolutely no bending, no twisting, nothing. And there was no exercise to be done at that time. I couldn't ride a bike, I couldn't do anything.' What should have been the start of an easier time for Smith, because after all the uncertainty he was finally on the road to getting better, was actually really tough for him. 'I think it was the worst part because even though I knew that I was recovering, I knew the actual recovery was still so far away.

'Had they said that I had to wear it for ten weeks, but on the eleventh I would be able to play, then it would have been easier, but I knew it was "Wear this for ten weeks. Then you'll probably have a month or two without it just to get your back used to not being supported totally by the brace – still no twisting, no bending, no anything, and after that, after maybe about five months down the road, we might let you ride the bike a couple of times a week. Then we'll start some light therapy. And a month after that well do some real therapy, and maybe twelve months from now, you'll be ready to go." So when they first put that thing on, it was ridiculous. I couldn't see twelve months down the road because I thought "How am I going to make ten weeks with this thing?"'

Of course the physical aspects were only part of the injury. For the long months that now lay ahead Smith had to come to terms with a new life. One he had never considered up to this point – a life without hockey. This in itself was scary. All his adult life he had been 'Randy Smith – hockey player'. His whole life had been dominated by the game. Everything he had done, he had done through hockey. It had become such a large part of his life that it had defined who he was. People treated him the way they did because he had been good at playing it. Now it was time to strip that part of his life away. Without hockey in his life, what was he? It was not a question he wanted to face.

'You talk to a lot of former hockey players, and they say that the thing they miss the most is the whole *aura*, of like, "I'm a hockey player."'

'People treat you differently. If someone walks up to me in the street, or I meet someone in summer, and they say "Oh, what do you do?" and I say, "Oh, I'm a hockey player." Then suddenly it's like, "Oh. You play *hockey*? Where?" Like suddenly they're interested. And I'll be standing with another friend and they'll say to them, "What do you do?" and he'll say, "I work for the phone company." And they'll go, "Um, that's nice," but immediately turn round to me again and say, "So where did you say you were playing . . ?" I mean, it's not the way it should be, but it's the way it is. And I mean, with the injury I wasn't the same person. It was a really depressing time.'

Of course, it wasn't just Smith who suffered. It was hard on his family too, particularly on his wife. 'I think it affected her because she knew how I was feeling. She knows how much I like hockey. She saw me have that taken away. Anything that anybody really loves that is taken away, well I mean, you realise what it means to that person. And she could see that I wasn't acting the same way around the house. I wasn't laughing or joking. It was a terrible year, I basically just existed. I don't want people to get the sense I was sitting in my house with a bottle of whisky, just going [pitifully] "Urgh, when's it gonna end?" – I was still trying to get on with the things I had to do – but it wasn't fun. I had something taken away, but then had that shoved in my face every day. The guys I was hanging round with are players. I had to go watch them play, watch them practise. Everything was hockey still, but I couldn't be a part of it.' Suddenly, everything he had known was under threat. 'I realised how much I loved hockey. I mean, I always knew I loved it, but to have it just all of a sudden taken right away . . . And there was always the chance that I wouldn't be able to play again. It was depressing. I mean it was just a horrible time in my life.'

Cruelly, for someone who had always been surrounded by teammates to help him out, Smith was very much on his own now. Everything in his life had been hockey, but that had never really been brought home to him before, because almost everyone he had known had been in the same situation. Only when it was taken away did he come to realise how big a factor it had been. When asked about what they love most about the game, hockey players will usually talk about being in a team, about being with their teammates, the closeness, the crack in the dressing room. It was exactly the same for Smith. They had always been a big part of his life, but now Smith found that he couldn't really look to his teammates for help. If he was no longer in the team, how could they still be his mates? Suddenly, Smith felt more lonely when he was with them than when he wasn't.

It wasn't that Smith's teammates were deliberately turning away from him, but awkward in his company, and perhaps feeling some guilt (needlessly) about the fact that they weren't themselves injured, they often wouldn't know what to say. And so, to an extent, Smith lost his teammates. 'A whole lot of the conversation amongst the guys always comes back to hockey. I mean you go out, say for a few beers one night, and you start talking, or you pretend to talk about things you think you know about – like what's going on in politics in the States, or whatever, and try and pretend you're an intellectual – but the conversation always comes back to hockey. And you're there thinking, "Well, I'm not part of hockey, so what am I going to talk about?" I mean, I'm injured, so I don't really know what they're talking about when they talk about that one time in Ayr, or whatever.'

To compound his sense of isolation, Smith had to watch from the stands as, without him, the Cardiff Devils celebrated their tenth anniversary by winning the league. Feeling like a stranger in his own team was bad enough, but to then see them carry on better than ever without him wasn't exactly the most comforting experience. I asked him how horrible this had been for him. 'It wasn't horrible from the standpoint that they won, because all those guys were my friends, and I wanted to see them do well. But to not be a part of it . . . In a way, it probably would have been easier had they not won it.' If the Devils had struggled, perhaps it would have been easier to have felt a part of things. 'Well, no one was saying like "Hurry back, hurry back." All the guys were genuinely concerned about me, and what was happening, but it wasn't a case of "Gee, hurry back, we really need you. Let's get the doctors on the move here. We need you back. We're not as good a team without you . . . " [Laughs] They just sailed right through and won it. It might have been mentally easier on me had they not won, but obviously I wouldn't have wanted them not to win it, or to take it away from them. They deserved it.'

Now he was out of the team, everything in Smith's life had changed. What had once been the place he loved most to go to – the rink – was now the place he felt most displaced. His entire routine was turned on its head.

Like a prisoner in solitary confinement, Smith now realised that he had plenty of time to think. For the first time in his life, he began to realise the extent to which hockey had ruled everything. As far back as he could remember, there had been the game. It had always been all he had wanted to do. 'You could ask most kids and they'd say the same, but when I was five, I *really* wanted to be a hockey player. Some kids would say "If I'm not going to be a hockey player, I want to be a fireman, a policeman and a cowboy . . . " But I just wanted to be a hockey player. My dad would say, "Don't you want to be anything else?" But that really consumed me. I guess I never really had anything to fall back on. I just had hockey. Hockey, hockey, hockey. And that was it.

'I always used to read about guys and they'd say, "One of the reasons I made it this far was I never went to the school dance at grade eight," or "I never dated girls," or "I never drank," or whatever. I'd read all these stories and think, "That's my story. It's just a different name." My wife and I started going out when we were 17 and she always jokes with me that I would never kiss her at my games or in public. I was worried about someone from the press printing "Randy Smith kisses his girlfriend!" – she still bugs me about that. I never went to any dances. My friends would come on by my house and say "Lets go to school, the dance is on . . . " – this is when we were about 12. I'd say, "Well I can't. The Bruins and the Pirates are playing tonight, and I want to go to see the game because we're playing the Bruins tomorrow night, and I want to watch Joe Brown to see how he does that one move, because I want to be able to stop him." It just consumed me.'

Now though, it was a time to stop and think. A time for introspection. It brought a few things into focus. 'With the injury, I realised how much I liked hockey, and how lucky I was to be able to play it for a living. Every kid I grew up with would kill to be where I am. I mean, I'm not in the NHL, but I'm making a good enough living, doing something I love, that I would be doing for free if I weren't playing for a living. I'd be playing on the weekends for Joe's Garage, for nothing, and having a couple of beers after the game, and laughing and joking with the guys, I mean, I'd do that for nothing. And I do it now, and I get *paid* to do it. The injury helped me realise that.'

Yet there was an irony here. Away from the game, he had missed it so much that it had hurt, but at the same time he had also begun to appreciate the fact that there was so much more to life than just hockey. I put it to him that although he had never yearned for the game so much as he did now, it was now less important to him than ever. 'Yup. Yeah. Yeah, that's exactly . . . all these things you're saying, I've had the same thoughts. I went from realising how good I have it, to realising that an injury, or your health, or your family, is more important than a game. I mean, if the doctors had said to me, "If you keep playing then ten years down the road, you're probably not going to be able to walk your daughter down the aisle when she gets married," then I would have said, "That's it. I'm done." The rest of my life is more important than the next 40 hockey games. It did make me sit back and realise that there were more important things in life than hockey. I had a lot of time to sit back and realise what I have. I have a great family, whom I want to spend time with. They're going to be with me the rest of my life, and hockey isn't.'

The injury had forced Smith to take a long hard look at things. He had faced things that most players put off facing until they are retired. With a chance to get back, he had a different perspective now. For any player, the question 'What am I without hockey?' is a big question. The truth may be uncomfortable, and a lot of guys just don't deal very well with it. Cocooned by hockey, they start to believe the hype about themselves. 'I think that guys get problems in later life. I mean they're used to the adulation. Even at the level we play at now, we're put on a pedestal. If you look at the world of hockey, I mean there's the NHL, and I'm in Britain. If you go on that scale, I shouldn't be getting any perks, or I shouldn't be getting people saying to me, "We think you're great because you're a hockey player." I mean, the guys who really *are* great are playing in the NHL. The guys who aren't so great are playing in the International League, or whatever – I'm 32, playing in Britain. I don't expect anybody to think I'm better than they are – but they still do.

'I mean you can go to a restaurant, somebody recognises you, the owner comes over and says, "Hey, wow. I was at your game. This meal's free." I mean, Joe and his wife are across the table, he's a plumber say, his wife's not working, and they're paying £40 for their meal. And I'm getting mine free because I'm a hockey player. I mean, I don't agree with that – although, if someone's going to give me a free meal [laughs] I'm not going to say, "Well hold on a sec here. I don't want it . . . " But, I don't agree with the way any athlete, or any entertainer, is put on a pedestal. I personally don't see how there's any hockey player in this world who can make £10 million, or whatever, when there's people saving lives. And we get paid for skating around and passing a pesky little puck around . . . ?'

But at the same time, it was still what he wanted to do more than anything. After putting up with the brace for ten weeks, there was finally a glimpse of light at the end of the tunnel. 'They said, "You can come back on, whatever date it was, and we'll tell you whether you can take it off." And I got there and said, "I don't care. You're taking it off!"' He remembers, 'They checked and said, "It's okay." And that thing was off.' The relief at finally being freed from his personal prison cell was tempered by the fact that there was still a long way to go. 'Even though they told me it was going to get better, it seemed so far away. But having had that time to think, I realised how much I wanted to get back. And when I thought about it that way, the recovery wasn't that bad. If it was going to take 12 months, but I'd be back to playing hockey, then it was not that bad.'

At season's end Smith went back home to Canada and was finally able to resume some training. The injury had clearly taken its toll, however. 'When I first went into the physio place they said they'd never seen a back like it in their lives,' he recollects. 'I'd lost all the muscle, everything was just gone. They said if they'd pulled a 90-year-old woman off the street she'd have more muscle on her back than I had. I had a spine and then, uh, nothing. So I had to get all that back, the movement back. I had lost about 7 per cent of the movement. There was therapy during the summer, and I started skating. There was a little bit of pain, but every doctor I ever saw said you can't have a metal disc and two screws in your back and not have some pain. I'll probably have a little bit of pain in there every day for the rest of my life. But it's not going to be enough pain to keep me from playing hockey. So I skated and was ready to go.' The question now was, were Cardiff ready for him?

Initially supportive, the Devils obviously, and understandably, began to have doubts about the kind of player that would be returning after almost 17 months of back trouble. At the end of his first season they had told him that, regardless of the injury, they wanted him for another two years, but when he missed the entire season, and he had still not seen a contract, he began to wonder. When he eventually saw their offer he was dismayed to see that it wasn't what he had hoped for. 'It wasn't just less money, it was quite a bit less money, and there were a few other things in there that weren't right.' Before signing, he decided to think about it, but before he could decide, the offer was withdrawn. Within days, he was off to Newcastle instead. After mentioning to Dale Lambert that he had been left without a team, Lambert had given him Rick Brebant's phone number, and the Cobras boss moved quickly to sign him. Medical checks were done, documentation produced, a contract offered and accepted and that was it. It had all taken about three days. After months of uncertainty at Cardiff, I wondered how relieved he had been. 'Part of the reason Cardiff weren't totally sure, obviously, was because of my back. So I thought, is that what the other seven teams are going to say? What do I do now? I was confident of my ability, and the doctors who had done this work and checked me out, were too. It was a relief to get the contract, but it wasn't as big a relief as maybe people are thinking, because I was confident that everything had gone okay. I didn't see it as any kind of gamble.'

But, inevitably, there were still doubts. It was going to take time for him to be like the player he had been before, but after so long, Smith knew to be patient. 'I knew it wasn't going to be back on the ice, a hat-trick and man of the match,' he says, but even so, he wasn't expecting the return to go the way it did. 'Everything went fine in the summer, then we played two challenge games against Bracknell and I felt okay.' Then, there was just this one time in training, we were going along, we did a couple of skating drills, and all of a sudden I felt something going on in my back. Then pretty soon it was all the same symptoms that originally had happened – I got pain in my legs, I couldn't move.' This was not supposed to happen. Smith thought the worst. 'They said they'd fixed the problem, but they either hadn't or it'd been re-injured, or another disc was damaged. My career would be over because if I had another operation, there was no way anybody was going to sign me after that, and if I had to play with that pain again, then I'd have to retire.

'I went to the doctor, the specialist I had to see was away, so I had to sit out some games 'til he came back.' It was a sickening, agonising wait, but thankfully the news wasn't as bad as feared. 'He came back, did a few little tests, X-rays, MRI, and what he attributed it to was just the lay-off. Even though I had been skating in the summer it wasn't the same as the games.

There was nothing the matter. It hung around a little while, the pain. But there's no way I could have screws in my back without pain, but then it slowly receded. The screws and everything were still in place, the fusion was good. It was just that after 17 months of not playing, my body just wasn't prepared for it. It was going to take time.'

And it did take time, but gradually, Smith clawed his way back, uncertainly at first, but then with a growing confidence. 'By early November, it was back, I would say. It wasn't causing any hindrance to my play. But before that it had been a mental hindrance. I would start a game or practice and not know how long I could last. When I went out on a shift I wondered if it would be the last one that felt good. It was mental, just eating away at me, but gradually I got over that. Now I know that when I start a game my back's going to last the whole time without any problems, apart from the odd twinge which I have to expect.' Though he has lost some of his speed, and a fraction of his mobility, Smith has made as good a recovery as he could possibly have hoped for. 'I'm as close as I can to being back to how I was after an operation like that,' he says.

But hockey is a rough game, and players have been known to key in on opponents' weaknesses. I wondered if he was scared that another team might try to deliberately re-injure his back. 'No. I don't think so. With smaller injuries guys might, but whether you're a hockey player or not, you're still human, and I don't think there would be a case where anybody would deliberately do anything. I think they realise how bad this was, and I don't think anybody wants to be the guy who ends a guy's career. If you knew a guy had a sore wrist or whatever, you might give him a little whack, but if you knew the guy had a broken wrist I don't think there's anyone in the league who would go out and intentionally try and hurt him worse.'

So now Smith is back to worrying about hockey again. At the time we spoke, his Newcastle side were having a horrible time of it, bottom of the league, bereft of confidence and just wishing the season would hurry up and finish so that they could start afresh. Normally, in a team that was losing so much, you would expect him to be suffering, but in light of everything that had happened I asked him if he felt differently to how he would normally in the same situation. 'I think, had I not missed a whole year of hockey, and then we'd struggled the way we did this year then it would have been terrible,' he admits. 'I mean, it's terrible anyway, but I think maybe, in a respect, it's not as bad for me as for other guys because I know how bad it is to not even be involved in it. I don't like being involved in a team that's not winning, but I like being on a team that's not winning rather than not being involved on one *at all*. That was the possibility I had. It doesn't make losing, or playing bad any easier, but . . . I'm trying to say this in the right way. I don't want it to appear that I don't care just because I'm glad to be there, but I realise that it can be taken away. I'd much rather be involved.'

To an extent, his injury had effectively put a ceiling on the amount of despair he could ever feel after a hockey loss. In the dressing room he'd be there with his teammates, and whilst they might be so sick with a loss that it felt like the end of the world to them, he would always know that it wasn't. 'It's a weird feeling. I hate to lose more than anybody, but, like you said, I could have been in that situation where I didn't even have the opportunity to win or to lose. I could have just been watching from the sidelines. So in that respect I'm grateful. These other guys have maybe never been in that situation – they've always been involved. It puts the game in to a different perspective to what I used to have.'

Realising now that he did once take it all for granted, and now deeply appreciative of what he has, Smith doesn't think he will ever take it for granted again. 'When I wasn't playing, I sensed that people around the rink were treating me differently. Even though they probably weren't. Even though I was still a member of the Cardiff Devils, I wasn't playing. It was just, "Oh yeah. There's Randy Smith." Whereas the year before people would want to tell you how great you were. There's so many little things. That's what I meant before about retired guys. They don't really miss going out and playing hockey. They miss hanging round the dressing room and talking with the guys. Going for lunch, girls following them around, guys buying drinks – just that whole lifestyle of you're a sportsman and people think you're . . . I don't know if they think you're *better* than they are, but they obviously appreciate what you do because they put you on a pedestal above everyone else. And that's definitely something you take for granted after a while. I go back home to Saskatoon in the summer, where I haven't played for 12 years, and I still have people going "Oh wow. That's Randy Smith . . ." I mean, that's going to end, and I don't know how I'm going to deal with that. I mean, nobody recognises you, or nobody cares . . . Like no one's going to be saying in ten years, "Oh, there's Randy Smith, the mailman . . ." or whatever I'm doing. I don't know whether I'm going to miss that or not. I wouldn't say I'm anxious to see, but I want to see how I deal with that.'

And the final irony of surviving a career-threatening injury is that when that career finally is over, Randy Smith is going to be a lot better prepared than most when it comes to building a new life after the game. It taught him not only to respect what he had, but recognise it too. 'A lot of guys, they're going to go their whole careers and not realise what they had. I had it taken away for a year so now I realise that you can be brought down to earth pretty quickly. These other guys will maybe have been playing for 20 years, then all of a sudden it's over. You always hear about so-and-so, the ten times MVP in the NHL, now he's a drunk or whatever, 'cos he just had everything. These guys would be just shocked to say, "Holy, I'm in the real world now. Nobody cares that I got ten goals for the Boston Bruins. I've got to get a real job." I was there. And I was close to being there for good. So that was when I was all depressed, then I started thinking, well, I'm getting a chance to go back to it. So it's not going to be so bad after all. Twelve months is nothing, when it could have been for ever.

'I appreciate everything now. Like I'm really stiff and sore after games and practice. Walking to the shower I get a lot of razzing from the guys, 'cos I look like I'm about 75 years old.

And Rob Trumbley gives it to me the worst. He says, "How can you do it? You look like an old man." And I said to him, "Trummer, I love every aspect of this game. I love everything about it. I like being on the bus. I like being at practice. I like being in team meetings. I like going for lunch with the guys. I like going to the rink early and taping my stick. And I liked doing all those things before, but now I realise . . . *it's a great life*. And I could not have that life very soon. And I could have not had it two years ago when this first happened." And he said, "How can you still be playing?" And I said, "Well, I like it. I appreciate it. I know what I've got. And I know that it can be taken away, so I'm going to enjoy it. If it means walking to the shower like I'm 75 years old, then fine." And the guys that aren't injured are thinking "You're crazy!" But hey, if I've got to walk like this, then that's a small price to pay . . . '

And so, for the time being, Randy Smith can look to the future. 'I'd love to be here in five years still playing,' he says, that Canadian kid in his voice still evident. But he's not that kid any more – he's grown up. And he's not just a hockey player any more. He still loves the game, but he knows that's all it is. A game of hockey. Not his whole life.

GAME OVER